Three More Archbishops
——— OF ———
Milwaukee

STEVEN M. AVELLA

Permission to reproduce the images in the book has been received from:

The Archives of the Archdiocese of Milwaukee (AAM)

The Archives of the Archdiocese of Chicago (AAC)

The Archives of the Diocese of Nashville (Courtesy of the Diocese of Nashville)

The Archives of St. Francis de Sales Seminary (ASFS)

The Archives of the Pontifical North American College (APNAC)
with permission of Msgr. Thomas W. Powers

BookBaby

Copyright 2024 Steven M. Avella

All rights reserved. No part of this publication may be reproduced, stored in a retrieval system, or transmitted, in any form or by any means electronic, mechanical, photocopying, recording, or otherwise without prior permission of the author.

ISBN: 979-8-35097-570-3 (soft cover)
ISBN: 979-8-35098-244-2 (eBook)

Library of Congress Control Number
LCCN 2024920359
Avella, Steven M., 1951
Three More Archbishops of Milwaukee
Steven M. Avella

To the Memory of Philip Gleason

CONTENTS

Acknowledgements 1

Introduction 3

Chapter 1: Samuel Alphonsus Stritch (1887–1958) 11

Chapter 2: Moses Elias Kiley (1876–1953) 75

Chapter 3: Albert Gregory Meyer (1903–1965) 105

Conclusion 127

Index 133

ACKNOWLEDGEMENTS

I would like to thank those who helped me complete this manuscript.

- The Archives of the Archdiocese of Milwaukee, Shelly Taylor and Amy Lisinski (AAM)
- The Archives of the Archdioceses of Chicago, Meg Hall and Charles Heinrich (AAC)
- The Archives of the Catholic University of America (ACUA)
- The Archives of the Diocese of Nashville, Tennessee, Erica Beatey (AND)
- The Archives of the Diocese of Little Rock, Arkansas (ADL)
- The Archives of the Diocese of Toledo, Ohio, Nicole Rhymes (ADT)
- The Archives of the Diocese of Trenton, New Jersey (ADTRE)
- The Archives of the Society of St. Joseph of the Sacred Heart, Carla Canady (ASSJ)
- Catholic Church Extension Society Papers, Loyola University, Chicago, Illinois, Kathy Young, Natalia Gutierrez-Jones (CCES)
- The Apostolic Vatican Archives (AVA)

- The Archives of the Pontifical North American College, Rome, Alberto Belletti, with permission of Msgr. Thomas W. Powers (APNAC)

- New Assisi Archives, Sisters of St. Francis of Assisi (NAA)

- The assistance of their Eminences Cardinals Pietro Parolin, Timothy Dolan, and James Harvey, Archbishop Jerome Listecki, Dr. Heidi Bostic, dean of the Klingler College of Arts and Sciences, Dr. Lezlie Knox, chair, Department of History, Marquette University

- The staff of the Apostolic Vatican Archives

- The Department of History of Marquette University

- Mr. Mark Schrauth, Salzmann Library, St. Francis de Sales Seminary, St. Francis, Wisconsin: Marelene Groff and Bonnie Yopps, St. Francis office services

- I am grateful for the hospitality of the Josephite Fathers and the V. Rev. Paul Hartmann, Staff House, National Conference of Catholic Bishops, Washington, D.C., the Jesuit Community of Loyola University, and Rev. Gregory Sakowicz, Rev. Andy Matijevic, and the brethren at Holy Name Cathedral, Chicago

- Dr. Joseph M. White and Rev. Michael Petrie who read this manuscript

- Dr. Anthony Bonta

- Jean Iacino who provided editorial services

INTRODUCTION

In 1955, Father Benjamin Blied, a professional historian and a former seminary teacher, self-published *Three Archbishops of Milwaukee* while he was the pastor of a rural parish in Johnsburg, Wisconsin. This and his other writings on Wisconsin Catholicism were an important contribution to local history.[1] Written in Blied's distinctive style, the book provided a lot of useful information about three relatively unknown prelates of Milwaukee: Michael Heiss (1881–1891), Frederick X. Katzer (1891–1903), and Sebastian Gebhard Messmer (1903–1930.) Blied was well qualified to write this work, as he had the ability to read German—the native language of these three bishops. In *Three Archbishops*, he combined what little documentary evidence then available with his own particular way of writing church history.[2]

Blied was *sui generis*.[3] A native of Madison, he had a troubled childhood, but studied at Harvard University and the University of Wisconsin

---

1. His most important text was a history of the Leopoldine Society of Vienna: *Austrian Aid to American Catholics (1944)*. This was self-published as were all his publications.

2. Only Michael Heiss was the subject of a respectable biography. See M. Mileta Ludwig, *Right Hand Glove Uplifted* (New York: Pageant Press, 1968).

3. Blied's biography was written by a widow who had become his devoted companion and admirer, Irene F. Franzen. See Irene F. Franzen, *Like a Beaten Anvil: The Story of Father Benjamin Blied* (1989). This work was self-published.

and earned his doctoral degree from Marquette University. Ordained to the priesthood in 1934, he spent a limited time in parishes until appointed to the faculty of Pio Nono College [high school] in St. Francis. According to his biography, he abandoned teaching history at Pio Nono in some dispute with fellow faculty members and resumed the life of a parish priest.[4] He and the other legendary historian of the archdiocese, Monsignor Peter Leo Johnson (1888–1973) held each other in mutual contempt. The Roman-trained Johnson had, however, the favor of the archdiocese and a secure seat on the major seminary faculty. He not only had access to many historical records but also scores of students who could translate German texts for him.[5] In 1960, Blied accepted a post on the faculty of Marian College in Fond du Lac. Here, too, he elicited a mixed reaction from the students and quarreled with the sisters over his living accommodations and their embrace of James Hanlon's innovative ideas about self-actualization.[6]

His unique personality—especially his penchant for blunt talk—blended with his expertise in professional historical methodology. His distinct way of writing included definitive (and sometimes cryptic) statements, often without reference to his sources. The author met him and attempted to interview him about his work on Katzer, but Blied kept interrupting the taped interview by insisting at certain points that I turn off the recorder while he confided something utterly harmless.

---

4. Franzen, pp. 56-58.

5. Johnson's longevity on the seminary faculty and his eccentric personality endeared him to many. As he aged, seminarians repeated his Johnsonisms and affectionately called him "Doc," as they did many North American College alumni.

6. James M. Hanlon, *Administration and Education: Toward a Theory of Self-Actualization* (Belmont, California: Wadsworth Publishing, 1968). Hanlon had been president of Marian College and had brought about a consolidation of the Catholic schools of the city of Fond du Lac.

He inherited a large sum of money from relatives and traveled extensively. In Fond du Lac, he bought his own home and made the city the object of his personal generosity. One of his charities included $145,000 for the beautification of the city's Lakeside Park. He also contributed substantially ($10,000) to the building of a circular chapel on the campus of Marian College named for the biblical figure Dorcas. One of his last works were sketches of the archbishops of Milwaukee that were supposed to be included in a 1976 *History of the Catholic Church in Wisconsin* authored by Norbertine Father Leo Rummel. For whatever reasons they were excluded as "not being sufficiently respectful."[7] This text makes use of portions of that rejected manuscript as a tribute to Blied's unique contributions to the history of the church in Wisconsin.

This book adds three more Milwaukee archbishops to the historical record: Samuel A. Stritch (1930–1940), Moses E. Kiley (1940–1953), and Albert G. Meyer (1953–1958). These three bishops were of different temperament and personality, but all had in common training in Rome during the early part of the twentieth century. This era was the high-water mark of what historians call a unitary Catholic culture brought about by four transformative experiences: the centralization of papal power, especially after the definition of papal infallibility at Vatican I (1871); the enthronement of Neo-Scholasticism as the official philosophy and theology of the church (1878); the papal condemnation of Modernism (1907); and the promulgation of the Code of Canon Law (1918). These developments effected a major change in world-wide Catholicism and had a profound impact on the development

---

7. Franzen's account of the rejection of the manuscript was, of course, respectful of the legacy of Father Blied. The texts he submitted to Rummel were short, but innocuous. Blied was forthright and even opinionated, but not disrespectful. Nonetheless, some bishops took umbrage at his blunt statements, one of them accusing him of "writing like the NCR" [the *National Catholic Reporter*, a liberal tabloid that annoyed many in the hierarchy]. See Franzen, 144-147.

of the church in the United States.[8] Historian Joseph M. White has noted that this was also a highly influential period for the formation of the clergy.[9] Understanding this wider historical milieu is of supreme importance in contextualizing the tenures of these three very influential Milwaukee archbishops. They saw the church and the world through a common intellectual lens. Yet despite their common training, these were three unique men and the historical context for each of their administrations was quite different.

Samuel A. Stritch, the first U.S.-born archbishop of Milwaukee (and the first of Irish descent) was born in Nashville, Tennessee in August 1887 and studied in Rome from 1904 to 1911. He was a pastor and diocesan official in Nashville, and bishop of Toledo, Ohio. He arrived in Milwaukee just as the Great Depression was blanketing the state of Wisconsin. He spent considerable effort shoring up faltering archdiocesan finances and energizing lay Catholic Action. His departure for Chicago in 1940 was widely lamented by Milwaukeeans who remembered his kind ways and appreciated his willingness to move among them with ease. He lived the advice he gave one of his successors in Milwaukee: "Don't run your diocese from behind a desk."[10]

His successor, Moses Elias Kiley, was quite different from Stritch. Born in 1876, he was a native of Nova Scotia, and did not enter the seminary until his late twenties. He studied in Rome and was ordained for the Archdiocese of Chicago, where he worked in a parish and then in archdiocesan charities. After a time, he returned to Rome where he became the spiritual director of

---

8. See J. Philip Gleason, "The Search for Unity and Its Sequel," in *Keeping The Faith: American Catholicism Past and Present* (Notre Dame: University of Notre Dame Press, 1987), pp. 136-151.

9. Joseph M. White, *The Diocesan Seminary in the United States: A History from the 1780s to the Present* (Notre Dame: University of Notre Dame Press, 1989), pp. 267-292.

10. This comment was related to the author by William E. Cousins, auxiliary bishop to Stritch in Chicago.

the North American College. He was appointed to the See of Trenton, New Jersey, in 1934 and six years later was transferred to Milwaukee. Kiley was taciturn and foreboding, but his thirteen years in Milwaukee were a period of relative prosperity, in equal parts due to his good planning and the revival of the local economy during and after World War II. Kiley ruled with an iron hand and was particularly hard on clergy. The last months of his life were spent in St. Mary's Hospital in Milwaukee where he died on April 15, 1953.

His successor was the bishop of Superior, Wisconsin, and a former St. Francis Seminary rector, Albert G. Meyer. Meyer was the only native Milwaukeean to date to ever sit on the bishop's throne in the cathedral of St. John the Evangelist. Born March 3, 1903, he was the son of a grocer who had a failing store on Warren Street on the near-east side of the city. He studied in Rome, was ordained in 1927, and remained in Rome until 1930 to finish a degree in sacred scripture. In 1931, he joined the faculty of St. Francis Seminary and in 1937 became the rector. In 1946, he was appointed the bishop of Superior, a diocese comprising the upper sixteen counties of Wisconsin. He remained there until September 1953 when he was selected to replace Kiley in Milwaukee. He spent five action-packed years in southeastern Wisconsin overseeing rapid parish growth, and the expansion of the school and seminary system. This was the greatest single epoch of expansion in archdiocesan history and required a pace that made him physically ill.

Each one of these men faced serious challenges presented by their times. Stritch had grave financial problems caused by the Great Depression. Kiley had to rebuild a burned-out cathedral, improve the growing archdiocesan seminary, and plan for a new orphanage. Meyer not only faced five years of rapid expansion but also the radical resculpting of the city of Milwaukee by the freeway system, the shift of the Catholic population to the suburbs, and the beginnings of rapid racial succession.

Their Roman training and uniform theological views provided a continuity to their era and a sense of stability to the experience of being Catholic. During their time of leadership, Milwaukee Catholicism was changing dramatically. Ethnic identity and its manifestations (churches, priests, etc.) did not disappear, but it waned as a defining feature of archdiocesan Catholic life. Replacing it was a cohesive Catholic culture that was underpinned by a fixed theological and ecclesiological vision.[11] These three prelates did not suffer questions about their roles and authority as bishops. However, the way each one exercised the responsibilities of their office differed markedly. They were all different in their views and approach to proper ecclesiastical governance.

Why This Book?

Much of the story of these three archbishops is related in my book, *In the Richness of the Earth: A History of the Archdiocese of Milwaukee, 1843-1958* (2002). But my respect for the work of Father Blied prompted me to build on his accomplishments. He was, like many historians, a complicated and even eccentric man, but his written work was, for the most part, very good. He was, in my estimation, a competent historian who knew the demands of the craft. Blied died in 1984.

But I had other reasons.

Even though it is disdained by current "influencers" among professional historians, I am a strong believer in biography. So is most of the reading public, who consume historical biographies and autobiographies in large quantities. Certain academics may turn up their noses at this type of history, but I still believe this genre provides a human face to historical narratives dominated by theory and statistics. Bishops were and are influential men who held real power. Who they were and how they were formed qualitatively affected their public life. While "dead white bishops" do not tell

---

11. William Halsey, *The Survival of American Innocence* (Notre Dame: University of Notre Dame Press, 1980).

the entire story of a local church, they have a presence and an influence that cannot be ignored.

This is also a work of revision. Some of the sources I use here were not at my disposal when I wrote the original work. Today the papers of these archbishops are much more accessible and well-organized thanks to the superb work of the archivists of the Archdioceses of Milwaukee and Chicago. I have also been able to use the records of the Vatican Apostolic Archives, which are now open to researchers. These are a particularly rich source and provide special insights into the lives of these men. Without papers ("dead people's mail"), there is no believable history. These new sources offer more perspective on their lives.

One other important source was oral history. When I first began working on these bishops in the 1980s, I had the privilege of speaking with many men and women who knew them personally. Reviewing the preserved transcripts of those interviews and comparing them with what I have read in the written sources has provided some fresh insights that were not originally available to me. A long career of reading, teaching, and lecturing on U.S. Catholic history and interacting with wonderful scholars has helped me understand my subjects better. This current work helps me see the past more clearly and understand what has brought us to the present moment.

In these sketches, to the discomfort of some, I have not held back from an unvarnished view of their strengths and weaknesses. An old Latin saying sums this up: *Homines non sunt angeli* (Humans are not angels.) I am no fan of what the great church historian Monsignor John Tracy Ellis called the "moonlight and roses" version of church history. Church history is not about old-fashioned apologetics—proof texting history as a defense against external foes. Rather, I have lived by the words of Pope Leo XIII: "the church has nothing to fear from the truth." The best apologetics is honesty, debate, and free discussion of all aspects of the church's life and leadership: the good, the bad, the ugly. Before they were bishops and literally invested with a status that commanded respect, they were also human beings with their own virtues and frailties. Stritch suffered from depression. Kiley was ill-tempered and at times abusive of priests and staff—yelling at them as though they were school children. Meyer was very introverted in a way that sometimes made people uncomfortable—even at a time when people did not expect bishops to be glad-handers. These observations about them are based in fact and do no damage to their often-unselfish work and ministry. Much of church history is a validation of what the Catholic Church prays as it honors the martyrs: "You chose the weak and make them strong in bearing witness to you."

After more than forty-five years studying the church in the state of Wisconsin and the Archdiocese of Milwaukee, this will be one of my last contributions to local Catholic history. I hope others will step forward to write the next chapters, correct what is wrong in my own work, and "bring the people into their heritage" (Deuteronomy 31:7).

—*Steven M. Avella*
March 19, 2024—Feast of St. Joseph

CHAPTER 1

SAMUEL ALPHONSUS STRITCH (1887–1958)

Archbishop of Milwaukee, 1930 to 1940

Samuel Alphonsus Stritch was born August 17, 1887, the seventh of eight children of Garrett and Katherine Malley Stritch. His father, a native of Ballyheigue, County Kerry, Ireland, had come to the United States in 1870. The elder Stritch was a bookish man who was once a schoolmaster (as was his father), who eventually settled in Louisville, Kentucky. Here he found employment first as a railroad worker and later as an employee of Major Eugene Lewis at the Sycamore Mills Powder Company in Tennessee. Lewis was a successful businessman and a highly esteemed public citizen who chaired the Nashville, Chattanooga, and St. Louis Railway from 1900 to 1917. He looked fondly on Garrett Stritch and his family, and one of the Stritch brothers was named Eugene Lewis Stritch. The family moved to Nashville, where Garrett worked in the central offices of the Sycamore Mills Powder Company. After Garrett's death, Lewis remained solicitous about the Stritch family. Samuel spoke fondly of him, as he did of many of his friends from Tennessee.

Garret met Katherine Malley, a native of Madison, Indiana, and of Irish parentage, and the couple married and established a home on Summer Street in Nashville, Tennessee. Garrett died at the age of fifty-six, leaving Katherine with eight young children. Little "Sammy," as he was called, was like his father—precocious, a bibliophile, and easygoing. The Stritch family were faithful parishioners of Nashville's Assumption Church, originally a parish for German-speaking Nashvillians, but a congenial church home for the Irish Stritch clan. For years it was administered by the German-speaking Precious Blood Fathers. Samuel was baptized by Father Clemens Roessner, one of the last Precious Blood Fathers to administer the church. The Sisters of the Precious Blood taught in the school. By the time Stritch entered first grade, the faculty had been transferred to the Dominican Sisters of St. Cecilia, a prominent Nashville-based community. These sisters, still active in the Nashville diocese and elsewhere, first stoked Stritch's lifelong love for quality Catholic education. He was next enrolled in Nashville's Cathedral School, conducted by Father John B. Morris. Morris's sister Ellen married Stritch's brother Thomas, making him a shirt-tail relative. Already as a grade school child, Sammy demonstrated precocious linguistic and reading skills, which boosted him beyond even the informal grade levels of elementary schools in those days. At the age of ten he was ready for post-elementary education. Yet while his rapid advance through school is often cited in biographical articles, Stritch was not by any means a genius or a polymath. He enjoyed reading, collected books, was unathletic, and seemed to have no other extracurricular activities. As Blied observed, "His hobbies appear to have been entirely intellectual."[12] In his mature years, he reflected often on his childhood in Nashville and memories of friends, colleagues, and places, reappear constantly in his later correspondence. Many who knew him remembered him fondly—especially when he rose in visibility and prominence in the American Catholic hierarchy.

---

12. Franzen, Appendix, The Wisconsin Hierarchy, p. a 11.

Assumption Church, Nashville (Courtesy of the Diocese of Nashville)

In Nashville he met three men who would have a profound influence on his life. The first was the local bishop, Thomas Sebastian Byrne (1894–1923), a former seminary professor and priest of the Archdiocese of Cincinnati who had become the fifth bishop of Nashville in 1894. Byrne himself had been singled out by Archbishop John Baptist Purcell for studies in Rome and remained there until ill-health brought him home prematurely. A stern but effective bishop in Nashville, Byrne recognized in Stritch a capacity for leadership. Stritch and Byrne developed a close personal relationship until the older prelate's death in 1923.[13] Stritch looked out for him and monitored

---

13. For more on Byrne see Thomas Stritch, *The Catholic Church in Tennessee: The Sesquicentennial Story* (Nashville: The Catholic Center, 1987), pp. 239-280.

his precarious health in his later years. He was later the administrator of Byrne's estate.

Another sponsor was the aforementioned Father John Baptist Morris (1866–1946), who had also begun his clerical education at the Propaganda and North American College in Rome in 1887. Ordained in 1892, Morris returned to Tennessee where he was given high-profile jobs: rector of St. Mary's Cathedral, private secretary to Byrne, and vicar general of the diocese. In 1906 he was appointed coadjutor bishop to the See of Little Rock—the first native Tennessean to be raised to the episcopate. He remained in Little Rock until his death in 1946. Morris was a strong advocate of Catholic education and founded a mission seminary and a school for Catholic teachers. Although traditional in his racial sensitivities, he created separate parishes and orphanages for African Americans. Catholic life in a Bible Belt state was anything but easy, but Morris kept his easy-going ways and retired as often as he could to his farm where he tended crops like a gentleman farmer. Stritch visited him as often as he could and monitored his declining health.

John B. Morris, Friend and Patron of Stritch
(Courtesy of the Diocese of Nashville)

Another important acquaintance was Josephite Father Thomas Plunkett (1866–1941), a native of County Cavan, Ireland. He was a relative of the Irish saint Oliver Plunkett. He came to America and worked for several years in the dairy industry in Chicago before entering the Josephite community and pursuing studies for the priesthood at St. Mary's Seminary in Baltimore. He was ordained in 1898 and began a mission for African Americans in Pine Bluff, Arkansas. In 1900, at the behest of Bishop Byrne, he came to Nashville where he opened a mission for Black people. In 1905 he opened another in Memphis. A thirteen-year-old Stritch served his first Mass in Nashville and continued to serve when he was home from the seminary. In addition to being a pastor, Plunkett was also a skilled architect and builder. Stritch venerated him. Plunkett was one of the steady influences in his life until the older priest's death in 1941. "When I returned as a priest to Nashville," Stritch noted at Plunkett's funeral, "I lived on terms of closest intimacy with my spiritual father. For many years he was my confessor and whatever progress I made in the spiritual life I may have made was due to his instruction and example…he was my friend and guide."[14] In addition to missions in Pine Bluff, Arkansas, and Jackson, Mississippi, Plunkett helped supervise building projects in Florida. He also built the house of studies for his own community in Washington, D.C. When he moved to Toledo, Stritch took Plunkett with him, as he did to Milwaukee and Chicago. In both cities he played a role in helping construction projects, especially the cathedrals.

After one year at a Nashville secondary school, Stritch presented himself as a candidate for the priesthood to Bishop Byrne, with glowing recommendations from Morris. Byrne took to a liking to young Stritch and agreed to send him for seminary studies in far-off Cincinnati, Ohio, where he attended St. Gregory's Seminary from 1898 until 1904. St. Gregory's, the preparatory or minor seminary of the Archdiocese of Cincinnati, was

---

14. Stritch Sermon, March 1941, Papers of Father Thomas Plunkett, Josephite Archives, Washington, D.C.

located on a fifty-seven-acre tract (later expanded to ninety-one) known as Cedar Point (today Mount Washington). The seminary opened in 1889 with twenty-three students and included six full years of study. The subjects were typical high school fare: math, science, history, Greek, geography, bookkeeping, letter writing, and of course Latin. When Stritch arrived, Father Henry Brinkmeyer, the rector of the seminary, "was respected as a man of learning, great gentleness, kindness, and goodness."[15]

The experience of this minor seminary was one of total immersion in the academic and spiritual life of the future priest. Intense study, daily Mass, meditation, and retreats prepared a young man for the ministerial priesthood. Socially, it cut him off from interaction with his siblings and girls, and the "normal" social life of adolescents.[16] Most of the students (the school population usually numbered in the nineties) were candidates for the Archdiocese of Cincinnati. By 1902 there were seventy-five students, the majority of whom were studying for other dioceses. In 1904, Stritch's final year, the minor seminary closed as the diocese adapted a program from the Diocese of Rochester to host a day seminary and have the boys remain home for their high school or classics education. Stritch was picked by his bishop to study in Rome.

At the age of sixteen, Stritch said farewell to his widowed mother and family and sailed to Italy and the North American College on the *Via dell'Umilta* in Rome. This would be his home while attending classes at the Urban College of the Propaganda, not far from the Spanish Steps. His appointment to Rome came as no surprise given his academic excellence.

---

15. Francis Joseph Miller, *A History of the Athenaeum of Ohio, 1828-1960: A History of the Seminaries of the Archdiocese of Cincinnati* (Cincinnati: Archdiocese of Cincinnati, 2006), p. 118.

16. See Robert L. Anello, M.S.A, *Minor Setback or Major Disaster: The Rise and Demise of Minor Seminaries in the United States, 1958-1983* (St. Louis: Enroute Books and Media, 2018).

Rome

Rome had a defining influence on Stritch's life and worldview. A relatively poor boy coming from the non-Catholic American South was likely overwhelmed by the experience of it all. The North American College had been under the direction and later the ownership of the American hierarchy since 1858. Scores of seminarians from various U.S. dioceses had begun their studies for the priesthood there—most of them considered to be the "best and brightest (at least so designated by this bishops) who were destined for higher office in the church.

The rector of the seminary in Stritch's years was a Philadelphia priest, Thomas Kennedy, who made substantial improvements to the cold and cramped buildings of the College. One of his benefactors was a former student and future bishop, John B. Morris, who paid to have new plumbing installed with individual bathtubs (a luxury not available for a long time.) Kennedy also installed low-wattage electric lights, which likely harmed the eyesight of the students but allowed them to read at night. The visitors to the college included an interesting array of religious and secular figures who sometimes spoke to the students. The spiritual director of the North American College was also a Nashville priest, Monsignor John Patrick Farrelly. From an aristocratic family of the old south, Farrelly had been in Rome for many years. Cultured and sharp minded, Farrelly was warmly admired by the seminarians and he no doubt took a special interest in one recommended by his diocese of Nashville. In 1909, Farrelly departed to become the Bishop of Cleveland, Ohio.[17] Bishop William O'Brien of Chicago, who knew Stritch well, insisted that it was Farrelly who saw to it that Stritch

---

17. Still the best history of the North American College, see Robert F. McNamara, *The American College in Rome, 1855-1955* (Rochester, New York: The Christopher Press, 1956), pp. 377-445. See Thomas Stritch, *The Catholic Church in Tennessee*, pp. 223-280.

was sent to Rome. Stritch maintained a close relationship with Farrelly until the latter's death in 1921.[18]

North American College Humility Street Rome (APNAC)

---

18. "Bishop O'Brien's Tribute to Chicago's Fourth Archbishop: Habemus Pontificem," *Extension Magazine* 34 (February 1940), n.p. Years later he directed the superior of the Chicago House of Studies in Rome to find and memorialize the grave of Mrs. Farrelly, the bishop's mother, who had died there.

Each group of seminarians were arranged in groups of ten called a *camerata* or a *cam*. These students would become close companions for the years in Rome. Each day the cam walked together around the Eternal City, viewing churches and monuments of antiquity. Stritch became an inveterate walker everywhere he lived, although his poor diet and smoking eroded his health over time. Each summer the seminarians repaired to a residence in the Alban Hills named *Villa Santa Caterina* where they spent the hot months of July through October.[19] Often, they received visits from Cardinal Rafael Merry del Val, a papal confidant who also vacationed in the nearby papal villa. According to Marie Cecile Buerhle's saccharine biography, del Val enjoyed athletic games (especially tennis) with the North American seminarians.[20] Pope Pius X, elected in the summer of 1903, was also quite fond of the American seminarians. He occasionally held audiences for them. He referred to them affectionately as "*I miei Benjamini*" (my Benjamins)—a reference to the youngest of the sons of the patriarch Israel. Pius X's pontificate left a deep impression on Stritch. During his years as a student, Pius X condemned Modernism as "the synthesis of all heresies."[21] Samuel would have been among the first clerics to take the "oath against Modernism" required by the decree *Sacrorum Antistitum* (1910). Stritch, like many priests of his generation, shared the pope's deep suspicion of modern scholarship, modern

---

19. One of the best descriptions of life at the North American College in the early twentieth century are the published letters home sent by Milwaukee priest Peter Leo Johnson and preserved by the Salzmann Library of St. Francis de Sales Seminary, Milwaukee. Johnson was slightly behind Stritch in studies.

20. Marie C. Buehrle, *Rafael Cardinal Merry del Val* (Milwaukee: Bruce Publishing, 1957), pp. 14-15. Buehrle also published *The Cardinal Stritch Story* (Milwaukee: Bruce Publishing, 1959). Both books are extremely hagiographic.

21. These condemnations came in two forceful documents, *Lamentabili sane exitu* and *Pascendi Gregis Dominici*, both issued in 1907. They strongly condemned any idea that church teaching or the church itself had changed over the course of centuries.

science, and democratic government. Despite a naturally positive personality, Stritch frequently inveighed against modern ideas and values.

Among Stritch's classmates, several became co-workers in the hierarchy, including another seminarian, Moses E. Kiley from the Archdiocese of Chicago, Francis Spellman from the Archdiocese of Boston, and Gerald Bergan, from the Diocese of Peoria. At the North American College, Stritch was appointed the head sacristan and prepared the altar for daily services as well as special events, such as episcopal consecrations. About 145 seminarians were jammed in the building. Even during Stritch's years, Rector Kennedy and others were already surveying areas on the Janiculum Hill where a new and more capacious college would be built later (with substantial help from then-Cardinal Stritch.) The North American College was damp and cold in the winter, had stone floors, and an indifferent cuisine. Living there was no Roman holiday.

Stritch and His "Cam" Front Row Middle (APNAC)

The Mind of Samuel A. Stritch

Studies in Rome instilled in young Stritch a worldview shaped by the reigning Catholic philosophy and theology of that day.[22] More than anything else, what impressed him was the neat symmetry, order, and vision of Neo-Thomistic philosophy and theology. His first two years were spent securing an adequate background in philosophy. The remaining four years of his study were devoted to the study of scripture, dogmatic theology, liturgy, and church history. As Blied recalled of Stritch, "He read voraciously and was a dedicated Thomist who preferred the text to the commentaries."[23] Philip Gleason best describes the impact of this theological vision: "In the cognitive sphere [where Stritch lived] an integrated vision had been achieved by St. Thomas and the Thomistic synthesis was the official philosophy of Catholics…everything had already been brought together at the highest level of abstraction." Because Catholics were grounded in this unitary theological vision: "the main task as perceived by Catholics…was the essentially practical one of bringing home to the faithful the full realization of what this unity meant to them personally, and the further take, likewise practical, of working out the implications and applying them to various spheres of social and cultural

---

22. The best explanation of the prominence of Neo-Scholasticism as the predominant ideology of Catholics prior to Vatican II can be found in the writings of Philip Gleason. See "The Search for United and Its Sequel," in *Keeping the Faith: American Catholicism Past and* Present (Notre Dame University of Notre Dame Press, 1987) pp. 136-151; See also the impact of this ideology on Catholic higher education: Gleason, *Contending with Modernity: Catholic Higher Education in the Twentieth Century* (New York: Oxford University Press, 1995) pp. 105-166. See also Gerald D. McCool, *Catholic Theology in the Nineteenth Century: The Quest for a Unitary Method* (New York: Seabury Press, 1977.) A book that deals with the practical implications of this theological dominance is William M. Halsey, *The Survival of American Innocence: Catholicism in an Era of Disillusionment, 1920-1940* (Notre Dame: University of Notre Dame Press, 1980).

23. Franzen, Appendix, The Wisconsin Hierarchy, p. a 11.

life."²⁴ Stritch deeply internalized this theological vision in his life and in his ministry. He was able to see, if not always clearly articulate, all things within the context of this well-defined theological synthesis. This, he believed, allowed him to think properly and rationally about any subject—theology, education, art, architecture, health care, priestly life, and so on. Grounded in right reason, humankind could then accept the revelation of Jesus Christ as expressed by the teaching authority of the church. Helping people have the same worldview was the key to his ministry, and he insisted that any educational program that took him as their patron and sponsor should have a strong philosophy requirement. When he became archbishop of Chicago in 1940, he mandated an extra year of philosophy for his seminary students at Mundelein. Among the professors he quoted often in subsequent years was the learned Servite (and future cardinal) Alexis Lepicier, a French cleric, who taught at the Urban College from 1903 to 1912.²⁵ Stritch's love for Thomism was recalled by Father Sylvester Gass, a canon lawyer who lived with Stritch for a year in Milwaukee. He observed, "Somebody used to say that before he came down to dinner he would look up a passage in St. Thomas's *Summa* and then start discussing it at table."²⁶

Yet despite his devotion to this system, he often got lost in a theological word-salad when trying to explain it. Blied noted tartly, "Writing lucid letters for the pulpit was not among his achievements." On the other hand, he was a popular and much sought after speaker. Blied also admitted that he

---

24. Gleason, "The Search for Unity," p. 140.

25. Lepicier and Stritch remained in contact over the years. When the cardinal visited his Servite confreres at their novitiate and house of studies in north Milwaukee in 1934, he had hoped to see his former student, but they missed each other by a day. "Cardinal Lepicier Visits Mt. St. Philip" *Catholic Herald Citizen* September 6, 1934, p. 2.

26. Interview with Monsignor Sylvester Gass, September 2, 1983, Milwaukee, Wisconsin, Archives of the Archdiocese of Milwaukee (hereafter AAM).

"had a winning smile and a facile tongue."[27] Unlike many other bishops, his rhetorical style seemed spontaneous and energetic—and indeed in many cases it was. Stritch was capable of bringing a crowd to its feet in applause—something few bishops or priests could do.

Stritch's Roman education included more than absorbing neo-scholastic philosophy and theology. The ambience of Rome had an evocative power that influenced his ideas of church order, art, and architecture. This ethos was best expressed by Stritch's schoolmate and successor in Milwaukee, Moses E. Kiley. In words that could have been easily spoken by Stritch, Kiley told the young men sent to study in Rome: "This is that which makes a student's life in Rome worthwhile. With intellectual advantages inferior to none of our American centers of learning, there is besides an education of environment and contact, a training for heart and eye and ear deep and far reaching in its formative influence and which nowhere else is to be attained. Monuments of all that is grand and glorious, in pagan as well as Christian civilization, meet you at every step. There are art galleries and halls of sculpture to delight the eye and instruct the mind; vast churches and rich shrines, which even from an architectural and esthetic standpoint command our highest admiration and esteem." But even better than these cultural monuments, he noted that, "work is done beneath the inspiring glance of Christ's Vicar on Earth and her basilicas and catacombs are shrines and so many open books wherein are written the brightest of the Church's history, perpetual incentives to the noblest thought and deed in emulation of those who have so gloriously gone before us in this divinest of all works: the salvation of souls."[28] Stritch was an Italophile all his life, able to converse in Italian so effectively that he once fluently translated for

---

27. Franzen, Appendix, The Wisconsin Hierarchy, p. a 11.

28. Moses E. Kiley, Spiritual Directors Conference, n.d. Kiley Papers, Box 2, Folder 3, AAM.

American pilgrims a discourse of Pope Pius XI delivered in Italian during a papal audience.

Rome also impressed on Stritch a reverence for the history of the church. What deeply moved him was the cult of the martyrs of the early centuries of Christianity. (His titular church in Rome when he became a cardinal was St. Agnes Outside the Walls—one of Rome's fabled virgin martyrs.) He shared the same sensitivity to American church history. However, the type of church history he learned in Rome was largely apologetics. This view of the Church's past emphasized the defense of the church from heretics, barbarians, the Enlightenment, and other social and political forces that threatened its unity, independence, and the purity of its doctrine.

He was ordained in May 1910 in the Lateran Basilica by Cardinal Pietro Respighi, the cardinal vicar of Rome. Stritch was only twenty-two when he presented himself for ordination and had to receive a special papal dispensation to be elevated to the priesthood at such a young age. He remained in Rome an additional year to finish his doctorate.

Nashville

In 1911, he returned to the Diocese of Nashville to take up his priestly ministry. Nashville was territorially a large diocese (41,750 square miles encompassing the entire state), but population-wise was small, with no more than fifty-five priests, twenty-nine churches, twenty-four schools, and a small Catholic population of 18,500. During all Stritch's years as a Nashville priest, the Catholic population of Tennessee never got much above 25,000, and the number of priests hovered around fifty-three (diocesan and religious). After a few months at Assumption Church in Nashville, Byrne assigned him to St. Patrick Church in Memphis, the largest and most prestigious in the city. St. Patrick's was founded in 1866, the same year a bloody race riot killed forty-five African Americans in the city. Memphis was a segregated city for much of its existence. Yet for many years, its leader was E.H. "Boss Crump," who amazingly allowed Black people to vote. St. Patrick's became legendary for its heroic service during a horrendous outbreak of yellow fever in 1873 that killed hundreds of Memphians. A new church had been erected in 1904, and it had a thriving school. Here he served under the pastor and diocesan vicar general Monsignor Dennis J. Murphy. Another parish assistant for a time was Father John A. Floersh, also a Roman student, who would soon be transferred to the Apostolic Delegation and later become the archbishop of Louisville. At St. Patrick's, Stritch met and became life-long friends with Father (later Monsignor) James Whitfield. Stritch made many friends in Memphis, later earning the status of an "honorary Memphian" from one of the city's mayors.

Young Fr. Stritch and His Close Friend Fr. James Whitfield
(Courtesy of the Diocese of Nashville)

At St. Patrick's, he worked closely with the Christian Brothers who ran a small college there and with one of the educators, Brother Maurelian Sheel F.S.C. Brother Maurelian was the life force behind the Christian Brothers College of Memphis, one of the premier sites of Catholic higher education in the American South. Stritch was impressed with Brother Maurelian, who placed a strong emphasis on proper preparation for Catholic school teachers. Sheel had strong supporters in Bishop Byrne and Father Stritch, and won their support for the teaching of Latin in Christian Brothers schools.[29] Byrne, too, was a forceful advocate for Catholic education, issuing a pastoral letter on the subject that Stritch invoked from time to time in his subsequent career.[30] He served in Memphis until 1916, when Bishop Byrne called him back to Nashville and handed him various administrative jobs, including serving as the secretary for education, chancellor, head of the Marriage Tribunal, and from 1919 to 1921 was rector of the Cathedral of the Incarnation.

---

29. For this bitter controversy see Ronald Eugene Isetti, "The Latin Question: A Conflict in Catholic Higher Education Between Jesuits and Christian Brothers in Late Nineteenth Century America," *Catholic Historical Review* 76 (July 1990): 526-548.

30. In the 1940s, Memphis erected a Catholic high school and wanted to name it for Stritch, who was by then a cardinal. Stritch demurred and urged that it be named for Bishop Byrne and alluded to his pastoral letter on education. Stritch to Father John A. Elliott, March 4, 1947, Stritch Chancery Files, Box C-F Folder 18, Archives of the Archdiocese of Chicago, [hereafter AAC].

Interior of St. Patrick Church, Memphis (Courtesy of the Diocese of Nashville)

The early years of his priestly ministry in the South brought into focus the basic contours of his adult personality. His nephew, Thomas, described his uncle as "fair and easy"—an Irish characterization. Kindly and affable, although given to swings of mood, Stritch had what his nephew described as a "sweet" disposition, "with only enough eccentricity…to give a pleasant flavor to his personality."[31] Unlike others trained for the priesthood in that era, Stritch was rarely able to bring himself to the uncompromising legalism and personal severity of some (including his successor Moses E. Kiley.) Some of his approaches were common sense. He lived in an environment where Catholics were a minority. He held strong principles, but his temperament was one of accommodation and gentility.

---

31. Thomas Stritch, in *The Catholic Church in Tennessee,* pp. 232-233.

His quickness of mind, friendliness, approachability, and the reputation he enjoyed as a scholar impressed Bishops Byrne, Farrelly, and Morris. In August 1921, thirty-four-year-old Samuel A. Stritch was appointed the second bishop of Toledo. He bade farewell to his family and friends in the Volunteer State and spent much of the rest of his life in the industrial north. However, he returned often, usually to reconnect with Bishop Morris, Monsignor Whitfield, and family members. On November 30, Cincinnati Archbishop Henry Moeller consecrated him. His friend and patron Bishop Morris was a co-consecrator. Samuel A. Stritch was the youngest member of the American hierarchy.

Toledo

Toledo would be a significantly different experience from the rural south. In fact, this portion of northwestern Ohio was a prime location for Stritch to learn the rudiments of episcopal leadership. Here he managed the robust growth of a strong local church. Formally established in 1910, the diocese originally consisted of sixteen counties in Northwestern Ohio. In 1922, Cleveland detached three of its western-most counties and handed them to Toledo. The now nineteen-county diocese consisted of a Catholic population of 122,500, 103 churches, twenty missions, and seventeen stations served by 182 priests. It had eighty-four parochial schools, and ten high schools. Stritch came to the city just as it was becoming a major urban center and its population soared between 1920 and 1930, surging from 243,164 to 290,718. For many years, Toledo was either the third or fourth largest city in Ohio. It also had a diverse spectrum of European ethnic groups in its general population. Toledo was a city on the move. As one historian notes, the growth of its industrial economy was rapid even in the depression-scarred nineteenth century. Toledo became a key manufacturing center of the Midwest, making bicycles and automobiles, and specializing in glass products of various types, from punch bowls to light bulbs. "By the 1920s," writes historian Timothy

Messer Cruse, "Toledo's rate of growth in manufacturing employment led the United States."[32] Stritch said when he departed in 1930, "I have seen Toledo throw off the last of the psychology of the village and take on the larger vision of the city it ought to be."[33]

In Toledo during the twenties, as elsewhere in the industrial Midwest, the city and its environs were experiencing a period of prosperity. This contributed to the explosive growth of the Catholic population. To meet this need Stritch approved a robust diocesan building plan of new churches, schools, convents, rectories, and various additions. Between 1925 and 1929 alone, Stritch approved the building of twenty new churches, twenty-three new schools, two orphanages, and five hospitals He created nine new parishes.[34]

The pace of Catholic life in Toledo was much faster than Nashville or Memphis, but Stritch managed to cling to his easy-going ways. He often slept late, answered the door of the episcopal residence himself, and resisted wearing ecclesiastical apparel unless he was in public. As bishop he occasionally had to make troublesome decisions or deal with so-called "problem priests." But here he learned to "temporize" or procrastinate and use his more tough-minded subordinates to administer correction or discipline. Throughout his life (but especially when he was afflicted by bouts of depression) he would practice masterly inactivity—deferring decision-making—often leaving subordinates frustrated. He retained the old guard of his predecessor, but as vacancies arose, he filled them with similar tough-minded decision makers. This included his secretary Father Max Walz, who helped him avoid unpleasant decisions. Toledo nonetheless was a good episcopal "novitiate." He met

---

32. Timothy Messer Cruse, *Banksters, Bosses, Smart Men: A Social History of Bank Failure in Toledo* (Ohio State University Press, 2004), p. 4.

33. Mossing 152.

34. "Quinquennial Report on the occasion of the ad limina visit of Samuel A. Stritch to the Holy See, 1929," Consistorial Congregation, Apostolic Vatican Archives (hereafter, AVA).

challenges that allowed him to hone the skills he needed throughout his long episcopal career. Stritch mastered the art of centralizing leadership, devoted time and resources to teacher preparation, managed ethnic differences, and tried to build a magnificent new cathedral. He was popular and even loved by priests, sisters, and laity.

Fr. Maximillian Joseph "Max" Walz, Chancellor, Diocese of Toledo (ADT)

Administrative Centralization

Toledo's nineteen counties required more orderly administration. Although not a canonist himself, Stritch retained a life-long interest and expertise in Canon Law. He used his authority from the "new" Code (1918) to centralize diocesan administration. His philosophical preference for the big picture—order, unity, and coordination—were also virtues of the businesses of the community. Catholic Charities had been organized as early as 1914, and Father Karl J. Alter was appointed the head of the new agency that centralized all the charitable activities of the diocese. When he was appointed to head the National Catholic School of Social Service in Washington D.C. (one of the main resources for professional Catholic social work), Stritch objected but eventually allowed him to go.[35] He would succeed Stritch as Bishop of Toledo in 1930 and have the task of paying off the enormous debts run up during Stritch's years as bishop and completing a huge cathedral.

Ethnic Diversity

Apart from the widened scope of his work, a more challenging feature of the Diocese of Toledo was its ethnic diversity. Irish and German Catholics had long been established in the city. As a rising industrial center along the Great Lakes, Toledo welcomed scores of immigrants from southern and Eastern Europe, including a strong Catholic ethnic cohort of Poles, Hungarians, and Italians. It also welcomed French-Canadians and Mexicans. Even though immigrant numbers would slowly decline (30 percent by 1890, more than 15 percent in 1920, and 11 percent by 1930), managing these ethnic groups

---

35. Stritch to John J. Burke, CSP, May 31, 1929, Archives of the Diocese of Toledo (hereafter ADT).

was a priority that tested the young bishop.[36] His default position was to accommodate as much as possible. Stritch approved national parishes, clergy, sisterhoods, and lay organizations. Stritch also paid close attention to ethnic balancing in appointments to church office.

One challenge to that diversity was the resurgence of the Ku Klux Klan, which targeted immigrants, Jews, African Americans, and especially Catholics. Toledo's chapter of the KKK made its presence felt when a large Klan march processed in front of his home in the summer of 1927. Stritch wrote angrily to one of the leading citizens of Toledo, Walter F. Brown, a prominent local lawyer in Toledo (and later Postmaster General of the United States): "Our concern," Stritch wrote, "is not with the Klan leaders or their pitiable dupes. Our indignation is for city officials who were solely responsible for the Klan parade passing the Bishop's residence and from such a line of march that no one in Toledo could mistake the implication."[37] Klan agitation would eventually diminish as the organization faded in the wake of serious scandals.

Teacher Preparation

As expected, he took a keen interest in the preparation of Catholic school teachers. These were mostly nuns, and for them he arranged for teacher-training institutions to meet demands for state certification. In Toledo, he inherited a healthy and growing Catholic school system of parochial schools, some high schools, and even a college run by the Jesuits. Father George Johnson, who would serve for years in the Education Department of the N.C.W.C., had overseen the development of diocesan schools. Johnson had laid strong

---

36. Stephen J. Bartha, "A History of Immigrant Groups in Toledo," (unpublished MA thesis, Ohio State University, 1945).

37. Stritch to Walter F. Brown, September 5, 1927, ADT.

groundwork for the upgrading and professionalization of diocesan schools. Stritch and Johnson's successor, Father Francis J. Macelwane, built on that.[38]

In 1922, Stritch issued a letter to teaching sisters of the diocese setting out rules and regulations regarding proper qualification for teaching in diocesan schools. His approach was summed up, "The Catholic teacher must combine in herself the ability of a devout religious and the knowledge of an efficient teacher…the Catholic teacher cannot neglect to submit herself to a thorough professional training."[39] In 1922, he helped create a Teacher's College, which was organized as a department of the local Jesuit-run St. John University. Housed in a city Catholic high school, it helped local teachers get coveted state teaching certificates. With the help of the Ursuline Sisters he helped found (and name) Mary Manse College, which prepared Catholic school teachers. In September 1922, the Ursulines welcomed thirty-six young women. This first class received their degrees in 1926 together with graduates of the Jesuit St. John's. Later, the college became a free-standing liberal arts institution and remained open until the 1970s.

Stritch also expanded the number of Catholic high schools in the diocese—mirroring a similar development in public schools. High schools now became *de rigeur* in diocesan plans, and the first Catholic coeducational high school in Ohio was founded in Toledo. This facility was expanded and renamed for him years later. Under Stritch, high schools in the diocese went from ten to twenty-four. Stritch pressed centralized high schools in the diocese where circumstances permitted.

By 1930, the Catholic population rose to 166,236. The number of diocesan priests had risen to two hundred and the diocese had 127 churches, twenty-three missions, 139 elementary, and twenty-four high schools.

---

38. Lawrence A. Mossing, *Giant in the Diocese of Toledo: A History of Most Reverend Joseph Schrembs, D.D.* (Toledo: Diocese of Toledo, 1987), pp. 83-92.

39. "To the Teaching Sisters of the Diocese," January 24, 1922, ADT. Also quoted in Mossing p. 14-15.

Cathedral Building

Toledo needed a new cathedral. When he arrived in the diocese, Stritch was informed that plans for a new mother church had been underway. St. Francis de Sales, the first Cathedral, had been an old Gothic Revival downtown church. Joseph Schrembs, the former bishop, purchased a tract of land west of the city on Collingwood Avenue and formed a new congregation called Cathedral Chapel, which was to be the nucleus of a new cathedral church. Cathedral Chapel parishioners donated the bulk of the funds for the new building and the old church of St. Francis de Sales was to be sold with the proceeds going to the construction of the new cathedral. Stritch altered these plans and kept the old church but moved the existing chancery building to the new site and set to work raising more than half a million dollars to fund the new cathedral. By 1925, the building of the cathedral began. Schrembs had engaged a Pittsburgh architect, John T. Comes, who had advanced a design that drew its inspiration from the Cathedral of Toledo, Spain.[40] When Comes died in 1922, Stritch partnered with architect William Tyler Perry and they envisioned a magnificent building, daunting in size, with high towers, elaborate woodwork, and carved statuary: in all a fitting tribute to the Catholics to the Toledo diocese. Named for Mary, the Queen of the Rosary, Stritch gave vent to every romantic image he had of the cathedrals he had visited as a youth. The formal cornerstone laying took place in June 1926, attended by cardinals enroute to the Eucharistic Congress in Chicago. To the delight of the city's Hungarian Catholic cohort, Cardinal John Czernoch, Prince Primate of Hungary, presided.

The huge structure went up slowly, relying on constant infusions of cash, mostly from the Cathedral Chapel, as well as a special cathedral fund. However, by early 1930 these sources were exhausted and there was

---

40. John C. Bates, Esq. "John T. Comes Catholic Architect 1871-1922" *https://dsc.duq.edu/cgi/viewcontent.cgi?article=1135&context=gf.*

still much to do. When confronted by the drain on the Cathedral parish resources, Stritch shifted the financing for the church to an unpopular assessment on the parishes. The new tax came just as the Great Depression hit Toledo's economy hard. It suffered one of the worst bank collapses in American history. The debts run up during the prosperous 1920s would haunt the diocese for a least a generation. Already in 1924 the diocese had, in addition to the cathedral, six parishes with debts of over $100,000.[41] The parishes could not pay, and the cathedral would stand unfinished for nearly a decade.[42] When Stritch was transferred to Milwaukee in 1930, he left behind $4.6 million in debt. As Stritch's successor, Karl J. Alter, wrote to Rome in 1934, "The economic crisis in the diocese is severe and prolonged. In the city of Toledo for example 70,000 individuals have to beg for their bread from public authorities. One industry that had 27,000 auto workers has been closed for four years. Twenty-five parishes are not able to pay their debts. All that deposited money in Toledo banks with one exception have lost their money."[43] It took Alter until October 1940 to finish the cathedral and retire most of the debt. As late as 1943, when Alter sent Stritch a donation for the Emergency War Relief fund, he added, "I wish it could be more, but you know our circumstances."[44]

---

41. *Relatio Diocesos Toltanan in America,* 1924. Consistorial Congregation, AVA.

42. Lawrence A. Mossing, S.T.D, *Young Shepherd in the Diocese of Toledo: A History of Most Reverend Samuel A. Stritch, Second Bishop of Toledo* (Diocese of Toledo, 1988). Mossing includes a detailed description of the building and adornment of the cathedral on pp. 63-107.

43. *Relatio Diocesos, Toltanan in America,* 1934, Consistorial Congregation, AVA.

44. Karl J. Alter to Stritch, July 7. 1943. Executive Records General Correspondence. EXERC/GO500/86, AAC.

Our Lady Queen of the Most Holy Rosary Cathedral, Toledo (ADT)

The experience of leaving all this debt behind truly depressed Stritch, and it may have been at this time that his occasional bouts of dark depression set in. If Toledo had been the proverbial "best of times" for the young bishop, it also turned out to be the worst of times. In Milwaukee, he would go from the frying pan into the fire.

On August 26, 1930, Stritch received news that he was to succeed the late Sebastian G. Messmer as the archbishop of Milwaukee. Toledo gave him an affectionate farewell—which included plaudits from local Protestant ministers, a Jewish Rabbi, and Rev. B.F. McWilliams, pastor of the city's Third

Baptist Church, the city's largest church for African Americans. After the band played "Dixie" as a tribute to Stritch's southern origins, he said, "Toledo represents something so unique, so wonderful in my life that I give up the burden with regret."[45] He always stayed in touch with Toledo and returned in 1940 for the cathedral dedication.

To Milwaukee

Accompanied by Milwaukee Vicar General Monsignor Bernard Traudt and Superintendent of Schools Joseph Barbian, Stritch departed Toledo on November 18, 1930, at 5:20 in the morning and arrived later that day in Milwaukee, where he was greeted by thousands at the St. Paul Station.[46] When he alighted from the train, he was escorted to a new black Cadillac that was a gift from the priests of his new jurisdiction, and driven to the episcopal residence on 2000 West Wisconsin Avenue. The next day he was solemnly "enthroned" in an elaborate ceremony with Cardinal George Mundelein of Chicago presiding and attended by scores of bishops and priests from the area. Shortly after these ceremonies he visited St. Francis de Sales Seminary where the rector, Monsignor Aloysius Muench, introduced him. He admonished the seminarians, "The priest must be a gentleman in the best sense of the word…." He next paid a call to St. Joseph School in Milwaukee where he highlighted the role of Catholic schools in facing the problems of the world.[47] A series of other symbolic stops included a New Year Confirmation ceremony and dinner with the orphans of St. Aemillian's Home and a visit to

---

45. "Honor Stritch At Farewell," undated clippings in Folder 32.1 Box Exec/CO6-4099, Executive Records, Catholic Bishop of Chicago Correspondence, 43816.07, AAC.

46. "Archbishop Samuel A. Stritch, Enthroned at Cathedral," *Catholic Herald Citizen*, November 20, 1930, p. 1.

47. "Seminary, Church and School Great New Archbishop," "Education Vital Archbishop Says at St. Joseph," *Catholic Herald Citizen*, November 27, 1930, p. 2.

the Apostolate of Suffering, a pious organization directed by a local woman Clara Tiry.[48] In mid-January he motored to the African-American school of St. Benedict the Moor on Tenth and State Streets. To the African-American children, he spoke paternalistically: "I have had orchids and roses and many other flowers, but the sweetest flowers to me are those of the cotton plant. I am very happy to have this institution under my care. Everything the Fathers tell me and everything the Sisters tell me are good. And you are good, aren't you?"[49]

Installation of Archbishop Stritch 1930 (AAM)

---

48. "His Grace Takes Christmas Dinner with Orphan Boys," Archbishop Visits Sick Apostolate's Headquarters Here," *Catholic Herald Citizen*, January 1, 1931, p. 2.

49. "Archbishop Addresses Children at St. Benedict's," *Catholic Herald Citizen*, January 18, 1931, p. 2.

Stritch's new jurisdiction spanned seventeen counties, included the state capital at Madison, and comprised 310,000 Catholics, 584 priests, 329 churches and stations, 187 parochial schools, and twenty-eight high schools. Milwaukee was an older, more-established archdiocese, and its major cities were all prosperous industrial centers. It also had a large rural sector. Ethnic consciousness was still strong, reflected in parishes, priests, religious sisterhoods, and devotional organizations. However, as in Toledo the intense ethnic identity of earlier years was waning as immigration had slowed considerably in the 1920s.

Like Toledo, economic conditions in Milwaukee and throughout the state were bad and destined to get worse. Unemployment skyrocketed as manufacturing operations in the major industrial cities of Milwaukee, Racine, Kenosha, Sheboygan, Janesville, and Fond du Lac were dramatically scaled down or terminated. Here as in Toledo, bank failures also contributed to the misery. In some of the most heavily urbanized areas in Wisconsin, the suffering was intense. By 1933, more than 51,600 Milwaukeeans had lost their jobs. Foreclosure and eviction rates more than doubled. By 1933, more than 34,000 families and individuals were on relief—representing twenty-one percent of the entire population of Milwaukee County. In the rural areas, especially the numerous farms and dairy operations, prices for commodities had been falling since the mid-1920s. Although Wisconsin had been in the vanguard of social safety-net programs, creating the first unemployment compensation program in the country and its programs of so-called "outdoor relief" operations helped to some extent, even these efforts fell short.

As public relief money ran out in the 1930s, it placed stress on private charities like the St. Vincent de Paul Society, which saw their caseload escalate to nearly 9,000 by 1933. Its small salvage bureau at Sixth and Walnut was frequently overrun by applicants for assistance, bringing the organization to the brink of bankruptcy.⁵⁰ Diocesan agencies such as St. Bernard's Home for Working Men on South Second Street served more than 214,000 meals in 1931. The Catholic Social Welfare Bureau was inundated with the needs of dependent children—many of whom sought relief in the diocese's over-crowded orphanages.

Internal church affairs were also in disarray, at least according to a negative report of the Apostolic Delegate, Archbishop Pietro Fumasoni-Biondi. He had inspected Milwaukee in 1929 and described a diocese with serious problems.⁵¹ Because Archbishop Messmer was frequently away from his job due to illness or international travel, the archdiocese was drifting. Vicar General Monsignor Bernard Traudt handled the day-to-day affairs of the archdiocese, but Fumasoni-Biondi reported that he was unpopular with priests, "who did not believe he has much intelligence and culture—he is simply mediocre."⁵² The buildings of the archdiocesan seminary were in bad shape and competition from new seminaries in Chicago and St. Paul were drawing students away from St. Francis. The seminary rector since 1921, Monsignor Augustine Charles Breig, was also an absentee administrator who was often away with Messmer as his traveling companion. Although the seminary faculty had been polarized along ethnic lines, they came together to oust Breig and in 1929 selected Father Aloysius Muench as his successor. Clerical discipline was at an all-time low, with many priests flaunting rules about public attire, associations with women, and absence from their parishes. Blied recalled that Stritch was concerned about clergy alcoholism and "imposed the pledge" on newly ordained priests. For the restoration of clerical discipline, Stritch issued a handbook in Latin that restated the rules governing clerical behavior, including public dress, and

---

50. Charts of the number of visits and expenditures spiked sharply from 1932-1940 See Albert Paul Schmimberg, *Humble Harvest: The Society of St. Vincent de Paul in the Milwaukee Archdiocese, 1949-1949* (Milwaukee: Bruce Publishing, 1949, p. 110.

51. *Visita Apostolica, 1929-1933, Delegazione Apostolica Negli Stati Uniti IX* Milwaukee diocesi, Posiz 97, AVA.

52. Ibid.

associations with women. Stritch forbade priests "to be out riding with women and girls, was a stickler for clerical garb and decorum" and "he startled his constituents with a galaxy of chamberlains and monsignors."[53]

Managing Fiscal Crises

But clergy misconduct took a back seat to financial issues. Here he faced the collapse of one of the major bonding agencies of the city, Hackett, Hoff, and Thiermann. This firm, which marketed many archdiocesan and parish bonds, unexpectedly went out of business in 1930. Its demise was assumed to have been the result of the stock market crash of 1929, but when partner Max Thiermann committed suicide by leaping out an eighth-floor window of Milwaukee's Goldsmith Building, a John Doe probe found that he had been embezzling money from the firm since 1926.[54] Responsibility for these bonds was transferred to the Marshall and Ilsely Bank. Many parishes carried a great burden of debt, and thirteen archdiocesan parishes were unable to make their interest and principal payments bonds. The total indebtedness was $325,000 in bonds.[55]

---

53. Franzen, Appendix, The Wisconsin Hierarchy, p. a 11.

54. Steven M. Avella, *In the Richness of the Earth*, (Milwaukee: Marquette University Press, 2002), p. 531. Stritch related the Hackett, Hoff, and Thiermann scandal in his report to Rome "Propter actus dishonestos praesidit sese in extremis difficultatibus invenit." *Relatio Diocesana Quam Reverendissimus Archiepiscopus Milwauchiensis Pro Quinquennio 1929-1934 Apostolicae Sedi Humili Corde Fecit,* Sacro Congregazione Concistoriale Relationem Diocesum, AVA. In this same report Stritch noted that he found a diocese in revolt against all discipline.

55. Three parishes: St. Jude's in Wauwatosa, Holy Family in Cudahy, and St. James in Kenosha, were in danger of defaulting on their debts. In his report to Rome, Stritch noted "Because of the economic crisis, some parishes and institutions were in trouble and had to beg for reductions in interest. In the case of parishes the treasures of the diocese had to be used." *Relatio Diocesana Quam Reverendissimus Dominis Archiepiscopus Milwauchiensis Pro Quinquennio MCMXXIV-MCMXXXIX Apostolicae Sedi Humili Corde Fecit,* Sacro Congregazione Concistoriale Relationem Diocesum, AVA.

St. James Church in Kenosha was a prime example. The church's parochial school, the oldest in the city, had burned down in 1923. The parish borrowed heavily to rebuild and re-open. However, when Kenosha's major industries began laying off its workforce, parish revenues dried up and the parish stopped paying interest on the loans. As the parish sank into debt, the pastor, an elderly priest who had been serving since 1908, broke down. Stritch was contacted by parish laymen and a local attorney who looked out for archdiocesan interests in the city who urged intervention. At a 1934 meeting with parishioners at his residence, Stritch directed the laymen to work on paying off the debt as well as deferred city taxes. He sent a young priest down to help take over the finances and then ordered the formation of a Holy Name Society. He traveled to Kenosha, celebrated Mass, gathered the Holy Name men at a breakfast, and told them to get busy raising funds to keep the parish solvent. He then ordered a Forty-Hours devotion of prayer to work for a solution. The efforts worked, as the Kenoshans raised enough to pay debts and the new priest negotiated and refinanced the debt. By 1936, the parish was solvent again.[56]

Stritch was especially anxious to keep schools open, at times imploring Mothers General of the teaching communities to allow their sisters to stay with low salaries and even with room and board as their only recompense.[57] Stritch soon came to rely on the services of Neil Gleason, a representative of the giant Northwestern Mutual Insurance Company, who helped him renegotiate debts. With the archdiocesan attorneys, he kept an eagle eye on

---

56. Walter Burke to Samuel Stritch, May 10, 1932, Samuel Stritch to Rev. R.J. Smith, February 14, 1933, Walter Burke to Samuel Stritch, March 4, 1933, Samuel Stritch to Rev. R. J. Smith, April 27, 1934, Walter Burke to Stritch, April 30, 1934, St. James File, AAM.

57. The Pallottine pastor of St. Anthony Church, Father Peter Schroeder, who had built a huge school building, paid the School Sisters of St. Francis in groceries until their Mother General Stanislaus Hegner objected. See Steven Avella, *Like an Evangelical Trumpet* (Milwaukee: Pallottine Fathers, 1998). p. 51.

the fine print of new financing arrangements. With only the sheerest of good luck did the diocese avoid bankruptcy, and none of its parishes or schools had to close.

Seminary and Cathedral

Parish finances were difficult, but ultimately the responsibility for them resided with the parish corporations. However, the archdiocese itself had bills to pay and the ability to do this was seriously affected by the economic decline of the region. Specifically, steep debts remained from the building of Messmer High School, which had opened in 1929. Annual assessments of the parishes—a mainstay of its support—fell to new lows. Additional burdens came with the need for renovations at the archdiocesan seminary and the rebuilding of the Cathedral of St. John the Evangelist.

Since the 1920s, the venerable but increasingly frail Monsignor Joseph Rainer had neglected the physical conditions of the seminary. Messmer replaced Rainer in 1921 and tried unsuccessfully to raise $5 million to fix the building. When this failed, he even offered to sell prime lakefront property to help fund repairs. Monsignor Aloysius Muench took over in 1929 and upgraded the academic standards of St. Francis. Muench shored up the finances of the seminary by creating burses or mini endowments for the education of seminarians. He opened the library stacks to borrowers, cleaned up the property, and planted the rows of stately trees that flanked the main entrance.

When Stritch came, he apparently made a grandiloquent promise to build a new seminary. Muench followed through on this and laid out plans to relocate the seminary to the western part of the diocese and away from the bustling road in front of it and from the girl's academy next door. Stritch rejected this idea. In October 1934, Muench proposed buying land adjacent to the seminary and building a new structure. But when he presented these plans to the archbishop, he again encountered opposition: "I spoke to him again about buying the 30 acres adjacent to the seminary grounds…We should buy this if the Seminary is to stay on this site." But the archbishop again refused. "He is afraid that the public might find out and the reactions would be bad, if we are buying up land in these times of distress." Muench insisted that with land prices being so depressed, it was the optimal time to buy. "Yet," he complained to his diary, "he would not take the chance."[58] Muench did not take the news well. A task-oriented, forceful person, he was often frustrated with Stritch and reported to his diary the sad details of the prelate's occasional bouts of depression and his slowness in making clerical appointments. Muench departed the seminary in 1935 when he was appointed the bishop of Fargo, North Dakota. Seminary repairs would be delayed until the next decade and the arrival of a new archbishop.

Stritch with Seminary Faculty (ASFS)

---

58. Diary of Aloysius Muench, October 19, 1934. Muench Papers, Archives of the Catholic University of America (ACUA).

In January 1935, disaster struck when the Cathedral of St. John burned, leaving only the walls and a weakened tower, but destroying nearly the entire interior. To this day, despite an arson investigation, no one has ever determined exactly what may have caused the conflagration, but the historic church was ruined. Stritch loved cathedrals and had shifted the annual ordinations of the new priests from the seminary chapel to the cathedral in his first year (1931). In truth, however, Stritch was underwhelmed by the Milwaukee cathedral, which dated from the 1850s and whose interior he thought cluttered and shabby. He noted to others that the interior was at odds with the elegant design of the cathedral tower, which had only been added in the 1880s. Stritch's nephew, Thomas, recalled that he was visiting his uncle when the fire occurred. As he rode with his uncle to the train station, he offered his condolences on the fire and remembered that the prelate smiled and suggested that the conflagration was "a blessing in disguise."[59] At first, Stritch may have been inclined to just tear down the buildings and relocate the cathedral to another large Milwaukee church.

However, he soon changed his mind. The urgings of his friend Monsignor Francis Murphy, the rector of St. John's, and the opinions of others whom he trusted, convinced him of the need to rebuild a larger and more "worthy" church. He began working with Father Thomas Plunkett and enlisted the services of architect William Tyler Perry of Pittsburgh, who had assisted him in Toledo's cathedral project. What emerged from their consultations was a magnificent replacement for St. John's—one that more resembled a Roman basilica, but with a much larger sanctuary. Perry and Stritch worked on plans and designs, which called for the use of the most expensive building materials. Both dreamed of giving Milwaukee a new Cathedral that would be a worthy successor to the work of John Martin Henni.[60] Stritch even

---

59. Interview with Thomas Stritch, July 15, 1989, Notre Dame, Indiana.

60. "Sketch Shows Beauty of New Cathedral's Interior," *Catholic Herald Citizen*, December 12, 1936, p. 1.

devoted a part of his now-successful "Archbishop's Fund Appeal" in 1936 to the rebuilding of the cathedral.[61]

Interior Ruins of St. John's Cathedral 1935 (AAM)
Burned Out Roof St. John's Cathedral (AAM)

But like the seminary proposal, these ambitious plans hit the cold, hard reality of local financial conditions and the needs of the poor. The cathedral had been woefully underinsured and existing coverage could only pay for the removal of the debris. Moreover, the mother church was always beset by heavy debt—most recently caused by building a new sister's convent in 1926. Stritch acknowledged that the cathedral had a shrinking membership due to reduced housing and competition from other parishes to the north, south, and west of the church. This had made finances a problem for many years. Hence, raising significant funds from the cathedral parishioners was not possible. But more than anything, Stritch placed a higher priority on

---

61. Editorial "Cathedral," *Catholic Herald-Citizen,* March 14, 1936, p. 4; "Charity Campaign Succeeds Spurt Toward End of Drive Assures Goal of $300,000," *Catholic Herald Citizen*, April 11, 1936. P. 1. The drive eventually netted $328,000.

the demands of charity, like the orphanages and other archdiocesan relief programs. Stritch reported to Rome in 1939, "The Cathedral 'per incendium destructa est.' Part of the external building has been restored but the work has been suspended without the money at hand."[62]

The Emergency Fund Campaign

Stritch faced significant debt in Milwaukee.[63] In 1932, he sought to shore up struggling finances by offering Archdiocesan Debentures to help refinance the indebtedness that had piled up under Messmer.[64] The next year, the demands of charity were even more overwhelming. The charities worried him the most—the orphanages, the care for the unemployed, the historic commitment to institutions for the deaf and blind as well as the home for the developmentally disabled in Jefferson. But the issue of funding the archdiocesan charities, particularly the three diocesan-owned childcare facilities—St. Aemillian's, St. Rose, and St. Vincent Orphanages–as well as the St. Vincent de Paul Society pressed hardest. In particular, the creditors of the St. Vincent de Paul Society were threatening legal action that would have pushed the Society into bankruptcy and seriously crippled one of the most effective agencies of charity for the archdiocese.

Pressed on every front, Stritch assembled an ad hoc committee composed of publisher Frank Bruce, brewer Val Blatz, St. Vincent de Paul chair Charles O'Neill, and seminary priests Aloysius Muench and Francis Haas to strategize on ways to shore up diocesan finances. For these men, the

---

62. *Relatio Diocesana Quam Reverendissimus Dominis Archiepiscopus Milwauchiensis Pro Quinquennio MCMXXIV-MCMXXXIX Apostolicae Sedi Humili Corde Fecit,* Sacro Congregazione Concistoriale Relationem Diocesum, AVA.

63. Samuel Stritch to William T. Perry, October 16, 1937, Cathedral File, AAM.

64. Samuel Stritch to "Dear Reverend Father," April 28, 1932, Stritch Papers, Box 2 Folder 1, AAM.

way forward was risky because the memory loomed large of Archbishop Messmer's failed United Catholic Campaign.[65] Nonetheless, this group urged the taking of a general special collection in 1933 called "The Archbishop's Emergency Charity Campaign." It had a modest goal of $75,000 that Stritch approved. He left organizing the appeal to a hard-driving local paint contractor, Frank Surges.

Stritch put himself front and center, pleading with the priests to encourage the generosity of the faithful. He laid out the grim statistics that in 1931 and early 1932 the archdiocese supported 2046 orphans and half-orphan children and ninety homeless men each day. It offered 7300 poor families services in free medical clinics. He pleaded, "Now it is not hard to understand our present plight. Our donations are few and less in amount on account of the severe financial strains of the times." He begged, "Now Reverend Father we turn to you to help us make our appeal."[66] Stritch kicked off the drive with a public rally and an appeal through the Catholic newspaper for people to step up and give. The workers in the field were the men of the Holy Name Society and the Knights of Columbus. To his amazement, the fund appeal, the first of six, succeeded beyond all expectations despite the bad economic times. With the influx of funds, the St. Vincent de Paul Society was saved. As one of the chairmen noted, if the collection had been meager, "It would have been necessary to close the doors of the Society if something

---

65. The Archdiocese of Milwaukee, in league with the Dioceses of La Crosse and Green Bay had attempted in the 1920s to raise $5 million, part of which would go to the seminary. However, the assessments met resistance from parishes, especially Polish parishes, who still nurtured grudges for being were taxed for the overbuilding of St. Josaphat Basilica. Reports in Archdiocese of Milwaukee Archives. See Avella, *In the Richness*, pp. 398-399.

66. Stritch to "Dear Reverend Father," March 30, 1933. Stritch Papers, Box 2 Folder 2, AAM. "Charities Campaign Opens Monday," *Catholic Herald Citizen*, April 6, 1933, p. 1. A copy of this letter was reprinted in the archdiocesan paper, "Charities Campaign Opens Monday," *Catholic Herald Citizen*, April 6, 1933, p. 1.

had not been done.⁶⁷" The next year he asked for and received $250,000. Often during these campaigns, he depicted himself holding a tin begging cup and insisted, "If we have two pennies in our hand, one of them belongs to the poor." To this day, although archdiocesan finances rely heavily on the assessment, great emphasis is given annually to this special collection for the seminary, education, and other pressing diocesan needs.

In 1936, he publicly prioritized the use of $125,000 from the $300,000 raised for the rebuilding of the Cathedral. Speaking from radio station WTMJ he pleaded, "This historical church and monument was destroyed by fire… we are asking in this campaign for funds with which added to what are in hand, we propose to build out mother church."⁶⁸ However, the cathedral plans stalled. Once the funds came in, he felt obliged to shift them to the orphanages and the St. Michael Priest Fund (a retirement instrument). He refinanced the debt on the Messmer High School bonds. He put off rebuilding St. Aemillian's Orphanage, which had burned down in 1930, although he did purchase land for a new building west of the city. In fall 1937, after receiving prohibitively high bids for rebuilding the cathedral, Stritch attempted to convince architect Perry to scale down the expenses by asking for a plaster interior rather than stone. Perry got upset and wrote to Stritch: "Three years of conscientious study have been given to these plans; and no Cathedral yet built has received such attention to the details of acoustic, lighting, or general requirements as has this cathedral. I believe we have been of one mind—to create a beautiful, practical, lasting memorial; to build otherwise should be

---

67. "Report of Meeting of November 5, Held for the purpose of discussing THE CATHOLIC CHARITY DRIVE," 1934, as Proposed by His Excellency the Most Reverend Archbishop Samuel A. Stritch, 1934," Circular Letters, 1933-1934, Box 2, Folder 2, AAM.

68. "Prelate Asks Charity Fund, March 16. 1936," Newspaper clippings, 1930-1958, Stritch Papers, Box 1, Folder 11, AAM.

the responsibility of others."[69] But the memory of the huge debt he had left in Toledo sobered him. Stritch explained, "my problem is economic." He explained to the unhappy Perry that he felt like "a working girl who longed to have a fur coat…but has to content herself with something that for the time will do." The problem was the continual indebtedness of the cathedral and the needs of the poor. He told Perry, "to assume a great indebtedness would be sheer folly."[70] The cathedral and the seminary would become the responsibility of his successor, Moses E. Kiley.

Although church-sponsored relief to the poor continued well beyond Stritch's term, the Depression taught Catholics the limits of private charity and gradually had to cede to the state the task of caring for society's unfortunates. Catholic Charities needed help and participated in the voluntary Community Chest appeals. However, as Milwaukee and the entire state tried to pull itself out of the Depression, it was clear that federal help—jobs programs, banking regulation, and other governmental assistance—was an important part of the state's recovery. Stritch did not accept this willingly—especially when it touched on areas that intersected with Catholic marriage rules, education, health care, and childcare. He wrote, "Unsafe minds today are advocating the substitution of public welfare departments to take the place of private charitable institutions and movements." Charity, he believed, was "the underlying foundation of our social fabric." Yet the Great Depression showed just how limited the private sector was in dealing with economic collapse of the proportions of the 1930s. The church needed money from outside sources. In the same message, he appealed for more help from the Community Chest Fund for the assistance of St. Charles Boys Home, a facility for troubled youth run by the Brothers of the Holy Cross. "We have a direct interest in the success of this drive for its failure would place us in

---

69. William T. Perry to Samuel A. Stritch, October 15, 1937, Cathedral File, AAM.

70. Samuel A. Stritch to William T. Perry, October 16, 1937, Cathedral File, AAM.

the necessity of raising a very large amount of money to sustain the participating Catholic institutions."[71] By 1934 and 1935, the first wave of New Deal programs was being phased in and provided some relief and recovery for various groups: the homeless, farmers, the unemployed.

The Personal Toll

Stritch lived simply. The generosity of others allowed him to travel on a pilgrimage abroad in 1932. When he was required to go to Rome for his *ad limina* visit in 1934, the consultors of the diocese held a fund drive among the priests, noting: "Since coming to Milwaukee, he has not taken a salary. A purse of considerable amount presented on his arrival here was dispensed by him in charity within a month's time."[72] Generous priests, many of whom were themselves strapped for money, nonetheless made this 1934 trip to Rome possible.

Stritch maintained his informal ways of doing business. For example, he was very inattentive to his clothing (or even his hygiene). As he had in Toledo, he answered the door personally and walked around the neighborhood. Stritch was a fragile person in many ways. His brushes with economic disaster in Toledo and Milwaukee scarred him for the rest of his life. He suffered from bouts of deep depression where he would lock himself in his bedroom and weep audibly for the sisters and the other priests in the house to hear. At a meeting held in November 1934, one of the charity campaign leaders reported, "We remember our Archbishop as he first came here, four-and one-half years ago. We can readily see that he has aged at least fifteen years

---

71. Samuel Stritch to "Dear Reverend Father," October 12, 1933, Stritch Papers Box 2, Folder 2, AAM.

72. Bernard Traudt and Sebastian Bernard to "Revend and Dear Father," March 1, 1934, Stritch Papers, Box 2, Folder 2, AAM.

because of his great responsibility."⁷³ Reporting more directly on Stritch's mental state was the observant Muench, who reported that Stritch did not come to the opening exercises of the seminary: "He was confined to his room with a bad cold. His is not a robust, vigorous constitution. Father Barbian told me he goes 'down into the dumps' easily. I have noticed that he is easily depressed by adverse news. 'He can't take it' in the phrase of the day." Stritch kept this from public view: "In public he does not show his spells of melancholy. He successfully hides the inner man by smiles and pleasantries."⁷⁴ In October 1934, Traudt confided to Muench, "He is very much dejected. Not long ago the A[archbishop] sat in his room, darkened brooding about something. When Msgr. Traudt came to cheer him up, he left his study and went into his bedroom. The Sister told Msgr. that she found the A[archbishop] crying in his bedroom."⁷⁵ These periods of depression made Stritch indecisive and slow to make critical decisions. Blied notes, "Archbishop Stritch could be exasperatingly dilatory."⁷⁶ Muench's diary confirmed this, "We feel that his nerves are worn down by his melancholy [contribute] to the lack of the power of decision." Muench further confided that Stritch spent so much time "keeping his ear to the ground to find out what people might think or say. Priests are beginning to mutter that he knows how to say nice things but does not do anything. It is time that his lack of making decisions is becoming more and more apparent. He puts everything off."⁷⁷

---

73. "Report of Meeting of November Held for the Purpose of Discussing THE CATHOLIC CHARITY DRIVE as Proposed by His Excellence, the Most Reverend Archbishop Samuel A. Stritch, 1934," Stritch Papers, Circular Letters, Box 2, Folder 2. AAM.

74. Muench Diary, September 18, 1934, Muench Papers, ACUA.

75. Ibid.

76. Franzen, Appendix, The Wisconsin Hierarchy, p. a 12.

77. Muench Diary, September 18, 1934, Muench Papers, ACUA.

For the rest of his life, he relied on the services of a psychiatrist named Ralph Bergen. A graduate of the Ohio State University, he followed Stritch to Chicago where he became an expert consultant for Catholic Charities on child welfare cases. His attachment to Stritch was deep and he even tended to him when the prelate was dying in Rome in 1958. Perhaps the most helpful Stritch confidant was Father Roman Robert Atkielski. He had been among the first priests Stritch ordained in Milwaukee in 1931. Enjoying Stritch's affection and admiration, "Romy" became for many years one of his closest Milwaukee co-workers. Barely two years after his ordination, Stritch tapped the young priest to serve as his personal secretary.[78] Atkielski performed this role and was later appointed chancellor of the archdiocese, but he also functioned as a sort of son/court jester for the moody archbishop. "Romy" could often snap Stritch out of his periodic bouts of depression and lecture the sometimes-heedless prelate about proper grooming while dusting off dandruff from his suit. Atkielski was also Stritch's companion for the long walks he took as the weather would permit. When Stritch left for Chicago in 1940, he seriously considered taking "Romy" along with him. Although this idea was abandoned, Atkielski made frequent trips to Chicago to spend time with the archbishop.

Other members of the official family changed as well. In an uncharacteristic decision, Stritch, allegedly annoyed by the advice of one of his priest consultants, Monsignor George Meyer, "to be good to Monsignor Traudt," did not follow custom and confirm Traudt in the office of vicar general. Stritch made the old war horse move from the episcopal mansion to the chaplaincy of Mount Mary College. Even the secular newspapers wondered

---

78. "Father Atkielski Named Archbishop's Secretary; Three Priests going to Rome," *Catholic Herald Citizen*, October 5, 1933, p. 1. Atkielski was at that time as an assistant at St. Stanislaus Parish in Milwaukee.

if he had been demoted. Six months later Stritch renewed his appointment.⁷⁹ Later he bestowed upon him the honor of being a Prothonotary Apostolic and appointed him to the pastorate of the prestigious St. Anne's Church on Thirty-fifth and Brown—a church that was under consideration to become the next cathedral.⁸⁰

Msgr. Bernard Traudt and Stritch (AAM)

---

79. "Msgr. Traudt is Appointed Vicar General," *Catholic Herald Citizen* April 16, 1931, p. 2.

80. "New Pastor, of St. Anne's Milwaukee," *Catholic Herald Citizen*, March 8, 1934. p. 1.

Yet Traudt's days of power and influence were over. He was eclipsed by a younger priest, Father (later Monsignor) Joseph Barbian. Ordained in 1903, Messmer appointed him the first Superintendent of Schools for the archdiocese. A strong-willed, no-nonsense type of administrator well connected ecclesiastically and in civic circles, Barbian did not restrict himself to school matters but advised Stritch on a host of issues. Barbian would be typical of the kind of person Stritch relied on much his life—administrators who had the task of saying no or administering discipline to priests—duties Stritch avoided when he could. Barbian died unexpectedly at age of fifty-three in 1936, but he was clearly the power behind the throne.

Stritch mostly projected a benign and fatherly persona and felt at ease among the people. He preached at the drop of a hat, becoming one of the most frequent public speakers in the American hierarchy. His topics were often on whatever subject he had been reading about prior to coming. A church dedication might get a sermon beginning, "I was reading Plato today..."[81]

His unfailing kindness and generosity were always evident in his personal correspondence. Particularly notable was his consideration for the emotionally fragile former Bishop Augustine Schinner, who found a refuge in the Motherhouse of the Sisters of the Divine Savior at 35th and Center in Milwaukee. Schinner's episcopal career had been a disaster. Appointed the first bishop of Superior in 1905, he sank into a deep depression which he blamed on the air quality. Released from this assignment by the Holy See in 1912, he hoped to become a missionary, but instead he was sent to found the Diocese of Spokane in 1914, where he encountered the same problems. Released from Spokane in 1925, he wandered from pillar to post to Bolivia, the Philippines, Michigan, and finally back to his hometown of Milwaukee. Stritch warmly welcomed him back to the diocese and gave him the occasional episcopal duty as his strength warranted. In May 1936, he arranged a surprise dinner for Schinner at the sister's convent to commemorate the

---

81. Father Gerald Hauser to author, November 10, 1983.

anniversary of his ordination. The bishop seemed pleased but retired as soon as he could from the party.[82] When the prelate died the next February, Stritch buried him with full honors at Holy Cross Cemetery.

Managing Ethnic Tensions

Historically, the Archdiocese of Milwaukee had been a cockpit of ethnic accommodation and contention. Ethnic parishes still flourished in Milwaukee. This diversity brought color and vivacity to the local church. It also brought bitter feuding and polarization. Under Messmer, relations with the Poles had at times been tense.[83] Stritch's experience in multi-ethnic Toledo served him well in Milwaukee, and he proceeded in these matters with sensitivity and patience. One flash point had always been ecclesiastical appointments. Stritch was keenly aware of how his Irish ancestry was perceived. He once dismissed the grousing of a group of Irish priests who complained that he did not make enough Irish monsignors as "Irish jealousy." Anxious to avoid any semblance of favoritism, he chose German or Polish surnamed priests for key positions in his official family as well as for coveted slots for graduate studies. Three men served Stritch as his personal secretary: Fathers Anthony Makowski, George Radant, and Roman Atkielski.

But he could not altogether escape the tensions of ethnic strife. One incident involved the relocation of an Italian church in Kenosha. Here an ambitious and charismatic pastor, Father Angelo Simeoni, decided to move the city's only Italian parish, Holy Rosary of Pompeii, to a new site some blocks north of the main residential and business district of the community.

---

82. "Surprise Dinner in Honor of Bishop Schinner Today," *Catholic Herald Citizen*, May 8, 1936, p. 11.

83. The bitter conflict between Messmer and the city's Polish community is described in Anthony Kuzniewski, *Faith, and Fatherland: The Polish Church War in Wisconsin*, (Notre Dame: University of Notre Dame Press, 1983).

This situation was complicated, with allegations of financial misconduct, bullying, and even at one point drew the attention of the Apostolic Delegate, Archbishop Amleto Cicognani. The episode revealed Stritch's approach to conflict: compromise and eventual capitulation.

Simeoni was a man of many talents—he organized church bands, encouraged sports teams, and roused the local pride of the city's Italians. However, he also could be mercurial and frequently withheld sacraments from people. (Stritch would later discover more than 100 unbaptized infants in the parish.) The pastor was unhappy with the existing church building, insisting that it was unsafe. He then found a new location on the north side of Kenosha and planned to build an elegant new church there. Simeoni's plans for the church ran contrary to the common practice in the Archdiocese of Milwaukee of building a school first and using its gym as a temporary church. Simeoni ignored diocesan policies and moved forward with his church plans, hiring a Florentine architect to design a new structure. He used monies he had accrued from years of fund-raising both in America and Italy. His plans nearly crashed when he lost some of this money in bad investments. To make up for the loss he sold the old church property to the city, who wanted to widen the street. This decision so antagonized many who lived in the vicinity of the old church that angry parishioners physically prevented the transfer of statuary and other church furniture to the new site. The new Holy Rosary of Pompeii Church opened in August 1932, but the battle was not over.

The disgruntled members banded together and took an option to purchase the old property from the city (which gladly accepted it during the Depression). When the dispute reached Stritch's desk, he sought to calm the situation by meeting with the dissidents to convince them to accept the new church. But they would have none of it. Stritch, fearful for the public reputation of the church, tried to placate both sides—halting the transfer of church statues and paying for new ones for Simeoni's church out of his own pocket. Eventually, when an Italian Baptist church eyed the possibility of taking over the old church, Stritch then forced a compromise by allowing two Italian parishes to co-exist: Holy Rosary, the Simeoni church, and the old church, now named Our Lady of Mount Carmel. He sent a priest who knew Italian to stay at the house of the old parish and hopefully mollify the dissidents. When he tried to remove the priest, the parishioners blockaded him, and a riot nearly broke out. He sent Monsignor Joseph Barbian with sheriff's escorts to extricate the "imprisoned" priest (who seemed to enjoy his moment of popularity). Ultimately, he pressed Father Simeoni to leave the city and resolved the issue "for the welfare of my Italian children" by permitting Mount Carmel to exist as a "mission" of Holy Rosary. He sent German Augustinian priests to both churches. They calmed the situation and eventually Mount Carmel eventually became a separate parish with Italian-speaking diocesan priests.[84]

Teacher Preparation: The Proliferation of Sisters' Colleges

As in Toledo, Stritch took a proactive approach to the cause of Catholic education in the archdiocese. He not only made sure that the schools remained open during the financial crunch of the decade, but as he had done in Toledo, he was determined to upgrade the quality of teaching. As in Ohio, teacher certification and the growth of Normal Schools provided an incentive for course work in pedagogy, student needs, and curriculum development. Public school teachers attended these institutions and attained certification. Stritch insisted on adequate teacher training for the religious sisters who taught in them. He was unwilling to send them to the local Downer College Normal School, which some suspected was promoting politically dangerous ideas. Stritch instead encouraged four communities of religious women: the Racine Dominicans, the School Sisters of St. Francis, the Sisters of St. Agnes,

---

84. The complex story of this Kenosha dispute is told in Steven M. Avella, "For the Welfare of My Italian Children," *Salesianum* 86, (No 1.) Spring/Summer 1991, 6-17.

and the Sisters of St. Francis of Assisi, to upgrade existing teacher training programs or create new ones. The sisters would conduct them during the summer months at their motherhouses. These programs eventually evolved into local free-standing colleges that supplied the needs not only of the sisters but helped the wider archdiocesan community.

Stritch did this in a way that would be inconceivable today. This was the case with the Sisters of St. Francis of Assisi. These sisters took care of his household, the seminary housekeeping, and taught in schools, including the boy's orphanage and separate schools for the deaf, the developmentally disabled, and the another for the blind in the archdiocese. In 1932 Sister Bartholomew Frederick, a member of the community leadership, was tasked with training sisters for grade school classrooms and to the order's St. Mary's Academy. Various options were tried: a summer program at the motherhouse, and, as a last resort, attendance at the intellectually suspect State Normal School. The best option of all was admission to Marquette University's summer sessions. When fourteen sisters needed extra training, Sister Bartholomew asked Marquette for a tuition discount because the community's straitened finances could not support it. When she petitioned Father William Grace, S.J., the dean of the faculty, in March of 1932, he put her off, insisting that he had to secure permission from a board that only met in October. Recalling this dilemma, she noted, "I did not know what to do. I asked to go to see Archbishop Stritch because he was a great educator. He listened to my story. He thought awhile, 'Your community is old enough and big enough to have its own college. Go home and start the college.' So, I went home and told Mother Celestine [Stark] , who was typing, that [Stritch] told me to go home and start the college. She looked disgusted but said that I should start the college. I was numb. I went to the chapel. I planned all night. The next morning, I went to Mother Celestine and told her, 'well I started a college last night.' I asked for three sisters to start the college. Sister Baptist [Ray] was to be the dean of the college. Sisters Joan [Reineher] and Letitia [Merten] were the other two. I told them what we wanted to do…All the postulants were to take the same classes. This way we did not need many teachers. This was our program for September."[85] Thus was born St. Clare College (later renamed Cardinal Stritch College), which met in the classrooms of St. Mary's Academy. Two of these colleges founded by sisters still exist, Alverno College of Milwaukee and Marian University of Fond du Lac. St. Clare/Cardinal Stritch and St. Albertus (later Dominican College) have both closed.

Also aiding the cause of a better educational system was a new Superintendent of Schools, Father (later Monsignor) Edmund Goebel. Following Barbian's death, Goebel took over and was the first professionally trained superintendent of schools, having graduated from the course of studies at the Catholic University of America in 1936.[86] A native of Caledonia, he was a former teacher at Messmer High School. When he took the reins of the Education Department in 1937, he was a force to be reckoned with in archdiocesan administration until his death in 1971. Goebel effectively centralized archdiocesan schools. He set up headquarters in an old Dominican convent called "The Calaroga" on Fourth and Galena Streets in Milwaukee. He worked with an appointed school board and was assisted by well-trained sisters of the various teaching congregations. He established a regimen of school inspections that paralleled the evaluations of the secular accreditation agencies. To assure the academic quality of school programs, he affiliated the schools with the Catholic University of America. With the substantial help of the sisters who assisted him, he produced textbooks that were required in the schools. Annually Goebel produced a statistical report and gathered the teachers in the fall for an annual convention. Goebel was an independent operator and was respected both nationally and locally.

---

85. Oral History, Mother Bartholomew Frederick, New Assisi Archives (hereafter NAA).

86. The origins of diocesan superintendencies are described by John J. Augenstein, *Lighting the Way: The Early Years of the Catholic School Superintendency* (Washington, D.C.: National Catholic Education Association, 1996).

Mobilizing the Laity: The Dynamics of Catholic Action

Perhaps there was no greater accomplishment during Stritch's years in Milwaukee than energizing the Catholic laity. Part of this was Stritch's oft-expressed pessimism about the social and intellectual trends of modern times. He frequently warned that modern society was abandoning its true anchor in religion. As he noted in a 1935 address, "If there is a single criticism that one would make of the greatest Catholic laity in the world—the Catholic laity of the United States—it would be that they have not a sufficiently intellectual foundation for their religion. They have not a Catholic mentality."[87] Giving them this "Catholic Mentality" would be the work of a re-organized and repurposed lay movement.

Stritch on His 25th Anniversary of Ordination (AAM)

---

87. Editorial, "A Frank Criticism," *Catholic Herald Citizen,* January 17, 1935, p. 4.

Drawing inspiration from Pius XI's encyclical *Ubi Arcano Dei* (1922), Stritch picked up the banner of Catholic Action. This European program sought to restore a more humane social order by establishing the reign of Christ over the world. It was conceived in part to withstand the secularized and anti-clerical trends in European governments which took control of education and marriage. In America, with its tradition of the separation of church and state, its vigorous public-school systems, and its religious neutrality, the program developed separately, although it used the name Catholic Action and openly endorsed papal calls for social reconstruction. Instead, it was advanced as a program of the bishops in which an active laity, under the direction of the pope and the bishops, worked to change society. At a meeting in 1931, he laid out his vision of Catholic Action. "Catholic Action is the participation of the laity in the work of the church which the present pope and his immediate predecessor especially have demanded as earnestly in the letters of Pius X…The Popes have not only spoken of Catholic Action, but they have also themselves engaged in its organization as in Italy and France."[88] The executive secretary of the National Catholic Welfare Conference put it even more directly: "Catholic Action to be specifically and definitely Catholic is not simply Catholic activity inspired by the motive of Catholic faith. Catholic Acton is defined explicitly as action commissioned by the Bishop—that is the Ordinary of the diocese and actually headed by him or his appointed representative…What makes Catholic Action is the direct authorization of the Bishops to particular action by which authorization he calls the laity to a

---

88. "Archbishop Summons Women's Council to Catholic Action," *Catholic Herald Citizen* October 22, 1931, p. 1. This explanation of Catholic Action was based on the definition given by Pope Pius XI in 1927: "The participation of the laity in the apostolate of the hierarchy."

participation in the apostolic mission of which he and he along is source and font for all individuals and all organizations in the diocese."[89]

This ordered structure of Catholic activity under his explicit direction fit well with Stritch's Neo-Thomistic sense of proper order and the hierarchy of truth. He defined and explicitly authorized Catholic Action and laid out the responsibilities of the laity. In a speech that brought men to their feet at a Knights of Columbus rally in 1932 he declared, "The day is past when the layman's debt is fully discharged by paying his pew rent…Great problems of modern society cannot be solved by a laity suffering an inferiority complex…"[90]

Stritch encouraged and authorized the development of lay Catholic Action along three lines: men's and women's organizations, youth groups, and social welfare activities. Stritch inaugurated his emphasis on Catholic Action by paying homage to Sebastian Messmer's earlier efforts promoting lay activism. In August 1931, he wrote, "I came to appreciate more and more his greatness of intellect, his foresight in matters of religion…" In encouraging lay action, "He was thirty years before his time."[91] In October 1931, he addressed the closing meeting of the Milwaukee Archdiocesan Council of Catholic Women (MACCW) at Mount Mary College. The MACCW had been first organized in 1920 under Messmer and had flourished under the leadership of several women, including Anna Mae Hackett and Katherine Williams.[92] Stritch was especially impressed with Ms. Williams, who was an attorney

---

89. Monsignor Michael Ready to Vince McAloon, National Catholic Welfare Papers, Box 138, Folder 16, ACUA.

90. "Archbishop in Stirring Plea for Catholic Action as K of C. Launch Educational Campaign," *Catholic Herald Citizen*, September 29, 1932, p. 1.

91. "Archbishop Messmer Father of Lay Action in U.S. Say Archbishop Stritch," *Catholic Herald Citizen,* August 6, 1931, p. 1.

92. Steven Avella, "The Milwaukee Archdiocesan Council of Catholic Women: A Brief Centennial History," private publication in AAM.

and later national leader of the National Conference of Catholic Women. Her activism advanced Catholic interests for working girls and women, the expansion of religious education, and the creation of summer programs for young people. She had been instrumental in acquiring an old resort on Lake Nagawicka in Waukesha County and turning it into a summer camp for girls.

The next year found Stritch addressing another important devotional group that was active in many parishes, the Sodality of the Blessed Virgin Mary. These groups had already coalesced into the Sodality Union of the Milwaukee Archdiocese (SUMA) in 1930. Under the leadership of Father Edmund Goebel and later Father Louis Riedel, this group attracted a spectrum of Catholic youth and played an important role in local religious instruction. They also sponsored a popular annual meeting in late summer that welcomed thousands of archdiocesan youths. This was just the kind of association Stritch loved and worked for in the archdiocese. In 1932, Stritch spoke to 3,000 sodalists at a ceremony at Gesu Church on the campus of Marquette University. "The church wants action not only a profession of faith," he told the assembly. He decried the "present distorted economic and social conditions" of the time and the "violence and radical political upheavals as a remedy for existing conditions." Recovery, he insisted, "can best be accomplished through intelligent social action."[93]

Although not formally part of Archdiocesan-sponsored Catholic Action, Stritch's favorite Catholic group was the Holy Name Society, a men's devotional society with parish branches, sponsored and advocated by the Dominican Order since the turn of the century. Stritch summoned the leaders to meetings at the episcopal mansion and laid out plans for organized and rejuvenated lay action. He encouraged them to build up the local membership and offer programs of interest to lay Catholics through a lecture bureau. The parish Holy Name Societies sponsored public devotions (such as the

---

93. "Active Catholics in Demand Archbishop Tells Sodalists," *Catholic Herald Citizen*, June 2, 1932, p. 1.

reception of a monthly communion) and helped mobilize local action by lobbying politicians on issues such as bad movies and salacious magazines and paperback books. Holy Name Rallies became a standard feature of the Stritch years as the group sponsored huge events that included devotions and a Stritch talk. In September 1932, 8,000 gathered in Kenosha for one of these rallies.[94] As he relied on Katherine Williams for his work with women's societies, Stritch kept close tabs on the Holy Name through a trusted layman Leo Dohn, a parishioner of St. Elizabeth Church on the north side as his go-to man for the Holy Name. Stritch later formed an office of Catholic Action led by Father Paul Tanner. The Holy Name men, aided by the Knights of Columbus and the members of the St. Vincent de Paul Society, provided the door-to-door workforce for archdiocesan fund drives. Thanks to their hard work, the ever-increasing targets for the drive were met and often exceeded. Directed by paint contractor Frank Surges for many years, they were a big help to the archdiocese and Surges got his share of diocesan jobs.

To the Holy Name Society, Stritch handed the task of creating viable, parish-based Catholic Youth Organizations (CYO). In a meeting of 3,000 Holy Name men at Gesu Church, he commissioned the men, chaired by Monsignor John Clarke, principal of Pio Nono High School, and publisher William George Bruce to help get this moving. Like the extremely popular program in Chicago, it was sports oriented and led by Marquette High School coach Peter Murphy. The CYO opened branches in all parishes, enlisted clergy support (mostly younger priests), and hosted devotional and social events for young people. At the organizing meeting in 1933, Stritch praised those who "are endeavoring so valiantly to make a genuine Catholic philosophy bear upon the world in which we live."[95]

---

94. "Eight Thousand at Kenosha H.N. Rally on Sunday. Hear Archbishop, Priest, Judge," *Catholic Herald Citizen*, September 29, 1932, p. 1.

95. "Archbishop Entrusts Boy Work to Holy Name Society," *Catholic Herald Citizen*, January 18, 1934, p. 1 & 8.

A more intensive form of Catholic Action came through the specialized movements founded by Canon Joseph Cardijn of Belgium.[96] These movements began in Europe as an effort to reclaim the working class in Europe who had been alienated from the Church. They put emphasis on the practical side of Christianity and encouraged people to look more closely at the deeper meaning of Catholic teaching. These organizations were more detached from direct episcopal leadership and took the command to re-Christianize society to a deeper level. The main groups were the Young Christian Workers (YCW) and the Young Christian Students (YCS), which formed "cells" based on vocation and age. These cells gathered weekly for prayer and formation in papal teaching, scripture, and liturgical theology, and pressed directly for social change. Following a simple formula based on an understanding of the theological virtue of prudence, adherents sought practical experiences where Christian values could be exemplified. "Observe, judge, act," was the popular mantra guiding these idealists. Weekly they would meet, discuss their respective workplace issues in the light of their Catholic values, and resolve to bring Christ to the situation. They were active in many American cities, especially Chicago, and they found fertile soil in Milwaukee, especially among communities of religious sisters, priests, seminarians, and laity. In Milwaukee, Father John Russell Beix, a professor at the junior seminary, became their chaplain and helped found a center in an old flop house which he renamed the Cardijn Center. To judge properly, many sought deeper education in Catholic doctrine, scripture, and liturgy as well as in-depth instructions in Catholic teaching on social issues. Here groups could meet, hear lectures, and share their experiences. They were never numerous but dedicated and focused on changing the world for Christ. Stritch regarded these groups warily, since they did not seem to rely on direct episcopal

---

96. A still-relevant work on specialized Catholic Action is Dennis Michael Robb, "Specialized Catholic Action in the United States, 1936-1949: Ideology, Leadership, and Organization" (Ph.D. dissertation, University of Minnesota, 1972).

direction for their programs, Nonetheless, as he often did, he simply allowed them to exist without much interference. His Catholic Action movements were much larger, robust, and properly directed.

Stritch as National Leader

Unity, uniformity, solidarity, collective action—these were watchwords of Stritch's social vision. From the local needs, Stritch also took cognizance of the wider needs of the Catholic Church in the United States and became active in the deliberations of the National Catholic Welfare Conference (NCWC). This body came into existence after World War I to coordinate Catholic support for the war. Catholic leaders came to appreciate the benefits of united Catholic actions, especially in dealing with the federal government. Despite some opposition, Pope Pius XI formally approved it. Since 1922 it was the official arm of the American bishops and was for many years directed by an Administrative Board whose membership rotated. Since 1934, Stritch was a regular member of this board, serving in one capacity or another—sometimes as the chair and sometimes as the treasurer. Here he often worked in tandem with Archbishops Edward Mooney of Detroit and John T. McNicholas of Cincinnati.

One of the most active arms of the NCWC was the Social Action Department (SAD). Chaired for many years by Monsignor John A. Ryan of Minnesota, it issued a progressive Program of Social Reconstruction based largely on Ryan's interpretation of Pope Leo XIII's *Rerum Novarum* (1891). This document called for social insurance, equal pay for equal work for women, and an active role for government in caring for the weak and disabled of society. In the 1930s, SAD was quite active in encouraging the efforts of workers to unionize and bargain collectively. Two Milwaukee priests, Monsignors Aloysius Muench and Francis Haas, were dedicated promoters of SAD's work and shared it with seminarians at St. Francis. In April 1933, close to 10,000 men crowded into the Milwaukee

Auditorium (a popular venue for Catholic gatherings). National Catholic Action efforts, spearheaded by Bishop Edwin Vincent O'Hara of Great Falls, Montana, found Stritch to be a welcome supporter. In 1933, more than five hundred participated in a Summer School of Catholic Action held at St. Mary's Academy in Milwaukee to study the implications of the encyclical *Quadragesimo Anno* (1931) of Pope Pius XI.[97] In 1935, O'Hara came to Milwaukee to lead a National Catholic Social Action Conference. Stritch strongly urged each parish to send four delegates and asked the organizations of the parish to cooperate. "It is hoped that this conference will present the most through synthesis of Catholic Thought on Social Problems and Ideals ever given in our country."[98]

Stritch embraced the papal programs of social analysis outlined in *Rerum Novarum* (1891) and its successor *Quadragesimo Anno* (1931)) To promote this vision of the Catholic social order, he even hosted a national Catholic Social Action conference at St. Francis de Sales Seminary in 1937. Stritch supported the main contours of Franklin Roosevelt's New Deal action for the common good, especially huge federal expenditures, which stimulated employment and had positive repercussions for local church finances. However, Stritch was never outspoken on issues of public policy even though he privately disdained the increasingly obstreperous behavior of the famous Radio Priest, Charles E. Coughlin of Detroit. Coughlin, from his radio perch in Royal Oak, Michigan, was a popular speaker. Even though he early on endorsed Franklin Roosevelt, he became critical of the New Deal and often misrepresented Catholic social teaching. He later became openly

---

97. "Eight Thousand at Kenosha H.N. Rally on Sunday. Hear Archbishop. Priest. Judge," *Catholic Herald Citizen*. September 29, 1932, p. 1.; "HNS Men Fill Auditorium for Rally," ibid. p. 1; "More than 500 attend Summer School of Catholic Action, ibid. August 24. 1933. Stritch had many rallies attended by thousands.

98. Stritch to "Dear Reverend Father," March 7, 1935, Stritch Papers, Box 2, Folder 5, AAM.

antisemitic and endorsed strange conspiracy theories about the administration.[99] Labor disturbances in Milwaukee and especially at the Kohler Company in Sheboygan found individual priests supporting the demands of workers, but Stritch remained publicly silent on these issues—except to warn of the perils of radicalism. As time went on, particularly with issues of foreign policy, he resisted public comment. He always insisted that the "mandate of his office" precluded him from too much comment on public policy. He was always a conservative southern Democrat and, as noted earlier, had a less-than-enthusiastic view of the growing influence of government—especially in works of charity.

The Archdiocese of Milwaukee slowly edged out of the Great Depression. By the late 1930s, Catholics, like other Americans, were turning their attention to events transpiring across both oceans, especially in Germany. Stritch also spoke out.

The Totalitarian Challenge

Adolf Hitler's accession to the chancellorship of Germany in January 1933 and his consolidation of that power the following year did not initially command the attention of Americans, who were wrapped up in the misery of their own economic woes. Pius XI attempted to maintain harmonious relations with the fascist dictatorship of Mussolini in Italy through the time-tested instrument of concordats (the Lateran Treaties of 1929.) He tried the same with Hitler, negotiating a concordat in 1933 which preserved the rights and status of the church in various areas—especially education. This was successful for a time but was soon flouted by Nazi leaders. In Germany, church leaders experienced pressure and active persecution of their public

---

99. For a solid treatment of the famed Radio Priest, see Charles J. Tull, *Father Coughlin and the New Deal*. (Syracuse: Syracuse University Press, 1965.) Monsignor Aloysius Muench also briefly engaged Coughlin.

activities, their schools, and special youth groups.[100] Likewise despite the so-called reconciliation between Italy and the Holy See, relations with "Il Duce" Benito Mussolini were often troublesome.

Yet as difficult as conditions grew for Christian denominations, the antisemitism and racism of the Third Reich was even worse. In 1935, the German government enacted the so-called Nuremburg Laws, which effectively deprived Jews of German citizenship. This decree not only affected practicing Jews but those who had converted to Christianity. The persecution of converted Jews—laypersons, as well as priests, monks, or nuns—set off a refugee crisis. Thousands of Catholics, as well as hundreds of priests and nuns, fled Nazi Germany to Holland and Switzerland. Their numbers imposed burdens on the ability of local churches to help them. Cardinal Adolf Johannes Bertram of Breslau officially requested assistance from the American hierarchy. This won a sympathetic response.

In 1936, the National Catholic Welfare Conference (NCWC) formed a special committee on refugees, headed by the German-speaking Archbishop Joseph Rummel of New Orleans. The Conference chose Stritch as vice-chair. They helped coordinate financial assistance and provided help in relocating hundreds of displaced clergy and religious. They also publicized the fate of refugee Catholics in the Third Reich—especially converts from Judaism. The central office of this committee was at the Leo House in New York, with a priest from that archdiocese as its executive secretary. Stritch, like the other bishops on the committee, was sympathetic but resisted any idea of bringing the refugees to the U.S. Nonetheless, he organized collections and wrote letters soliciting funds.

Stritch's normal reticence to speak bluntly about public policy was certainly tested when his episcopal colleague to the south, Cardinal George

---

100. The story of the clash of the Church with the antisemitic policies of Italy and Germany is expertly told in David Kertzer, *The Pope and Mussolini* (Random House 2014); *The Pope at War* (Penguin/Random House, 2022).

Mundelein, made international headlines in 1937 by referring to Hitler as "an Austrian paper hanger, and a poor one at that…"[101] Reports on the plight of the refugees came to him through the NCWC committee and the newspapers.

Initially, the cautious Stritch walked a fine line when discussing German issues. He was always careful to distinguish the German people from the Nazis. However, when the Nazis took over Austria in March 1938, a move supported by Cardinal Theodore Innitzer of Vienna, Stritch noted critically, "I had hoped for something more from Cardinal Innitzer, who is a brilliant man and my friend. Maybe he was too confident, but then one must make every sacrifice for religion. I had hope there would come about an understanding and that the nazis would see the light. In their politics we have no controversy with them." Stritch naively credited Hitler and his henchman with far more cultural sensitivity to law and human rights than their actions warranted. "If only they would see that the [union of the] Gothic mind, Roman law, and the church gave us the great thing of Teutonic culture. All these things are congenial. Unless they are united, we shall go back to the days that Tacitus described. I am praying that when he goes to Rome 'Der Fuehrer' will kneel at the feet of the Holy Father and listen to wisdom."[102]

But as time went on, Stritch echoed the public disdain of Pope Pius XI, who denounced the Nazis as aggressive pagans who wanted to replace Christianity with the worship of the state. By October 1938, after Hitler had bullied England and France into betraying Czechoslovakia during the Munich Crisis, Stritch lent his name to a statement that decried the "indirect means" by which Nazis were attempting to abolish the Catholic Church. He worried especially about the persecution of Jews, including those who had

---

101. Edward R. Kantowicz *Corporation Sole: Cardinal Mundelein and Chicago Catholicism* (Notre Dame: University of Notre Dame Press, 1983), pp. 224-225.

102. Stritch to Joseph A. Rummel, April 19, 1938, "German Refugee Problem 1937-1939," Stritch Papers, Box 1, Folder 6, AAM.

converted to Catholicism. In a widely publicized letter to Rabbi Joseph Baron of Temple Emanu-el, a respected leader of Milwaukee's Jewish community, Stritch declared, "Now it is all too true that your people have been the victim of a wicked movement which distorts truth and gilds falsehood. Against this wicked thing it is our duty to protest for we claim to be followers of Him who proclaimed 'I am the Truth.' Perhaps we entertain a more intimate sympathy with you these days for Catholics too are victims of vile propaganda…You may be assured that I am always sympathetic to every effort to promote the universal recognition of human rights…"[103]

His strongest words came in the wake of the *Kristallnacht* vandalism of Jewish businesses in Germany on the night November 9-10, 1938. Stritch spoke out in November 1938 at the fiftieth anniversary of the German parish of St. Boniface Church in Milwaukee, denouncing Nazi tyranny: "This paganism…the same concept of life found in the senseless leaders of Nazi Germany…in Germany, men are persecuted because of their religion, thrown into concentration camps for daring to follow their consciences." Singling out the plight of the Jews he declared, "We see a spectacle that makes our hearts bleed, the inhuman persecution of the Jewish people there. All these things that Christianity has stood for; these leaders have cast to the wind."[104] In January 1939, he issued a plea to the people of the archdiocese to help the refugees from Nazi tyranny. He scored National Socialism and its anti-religious program as "at its core a philosophy of life in utter contradiction with Christianity and sound reason." His plea for generosity had unique local twist. "When we were but a foreign mission, how many noble priests came to us willingly and cheerfully from Germany and Austria to minister to us…

---

103. Quoted in Buehrle, *The Cardinal Stritch Story*, p. 45.

104. *Catholic Herald Citizen* November 9, 1938.

were not many of the Sisterhoods that came to us from Germany?"[105] In this appeal in February 1939, he managed to raise $8,000. The actual outbreak of war in Europe in September 1939 found Stritch leading a huge candlelight prayer vigil sponsored by the Holy Name Society. Nine days after Hitler's *blitzkrieg* savaged Poland, more than 60,000 gathered at Marquette Stadium to pray for peace.

A month after the invasion of Poland, Cardinal George Mundelein of Chicago died. This set in motion two events: one was the appointment of Archbishop Stritch to the See of Chicago. The second was the promotion of Bishop Moses E. Kiley of Trenton to succeed him in Milwaukee. The Catholics of Milwaukee loved Stritch. When he celebrated his twenty-fifth anniversary of priestly ordination in 1935, thousands turned out to fete him in the Milwaukee Auditorium. In early 1940, thousands of Milwaukeeans again gathered to say farewell to Stritch, whom they had taken to their hearts. Stritch always cherished warm memories and friendships from his days in Milwaukee.

As when he departed Toledo, there was much left undone. The Cathedral of St. John the Evangelist was still unfinished, and his successor was enthroned in Gesu Church. Plans for the reform of the seminary and the upgrading of its buildings were waiting, and St. Aemillian's Orphanage was still in temporary quarters. His successor would implement all these projects and Stritch would go on to the last and most challenging appointment of his career: the large and complex Archdiocese of Chicago.

---

105. Stritch to "Dearly Beloved in Christ," January 31, 1939, Stritch Papers, Box 2, Folder 6, AAM.

+ Sebastian G. Messmer
Archbishop of Milwaukee

CHAPTER 2

MOSES ELIAS KILEY (1876–1953)

Archbishop of Milwaukee, 1940–1953

Although they shared a common Irish lineage, Moses E. Kiley and Samuel A. Stritch could not have been more different. Kiley towered at six foot, six inches, while Stritch was short and pudgy. Kiley was a workaholic and a micromanager, while Stritch delegated much to his staffers and enjoyed a comparatively leisurely lifestyle. Stritch put people at ease, while Kiley was formal and remote. Both men had a sentimental streak, but Kiley's emerged only rarely. Stritch had a more fertile and creative intellect and could speak well. Kiley was plodding and legalistic in character. The most charitable way of describing his public discourse was that it was less effective than his predecessor. Yet despite their temperamental and intellectual differences, the two men were friends from their student days in Rome and in occasional interactions in the hierarchy. When the See of Chicago came open in 1939, they were rivals for the appointment.[106]

---

106. "Chicago" *Delegazione Apostolic Negli Stati Uniti, America IV, provista della arcidiocese Liste Episcopale 732 376/39-Morte Cardinal Mundelein*, AVA.

Moses Elias Kiley, one of nine children of Nova Scotians John and Margaret McGarry Kiley, was born November 13, 1876, in Margaree on the western slope of Cape Breton Island in Nova Scotia.[107] Moses (or "Mose" as he was known) was named for his uncle, Father Moses McGarry, a priest of the Congregation of the Holy Cross. The McGarrys and the Kileys were a close-knit family. The Kileys farmed around the city of Baddeck, Nova Scotia, and were a serious and sober-minded lot. As his elder brothers moved away to pursue their own careers, Mose became an indispensable farm hand. He reached full height by the age of fifteen. In 1894, the family pulled up stakes and moved to Somerville, Massachusetts, where some of the older boys had established a successful carriage factory. Moses went to work with one of his McGarry cousins, becoming a capable wood worker—a skill he used in his priestly career—while his cousin did the iron work. Moses had other jobs—for example, as an errand boy in a Boston department store. Thrifty and disciplined, he supported himself and saved for future education. When in college, Moses went home during the summer and worked as a security guard and as a motorman on the Boston Transit Lines (he proudly kept his badge for his whole life). These years of manual labor left a mark on Kiley, and he referred to them often. There were no end-runs around hard work, discipline, and order. When he was installed as archbishop of Milwaukee, his sister Mary burbled to the local press, "He never had any hobby outside of [his] work."[108] Life for him was about accomplishing tasks. To do this he insisted that he know with clarity what he was supposed to do. Being faithful to his duty was the paramount direction of his life.

---

107. There is no record of his naturalization in his papers. Presumably, this happened when the family moved to Massachusetts.

108. "Kileys Here for Rites Recalls Childhood Days," clipping from *Milwaukee Sentinel*, March 28, 1940, Kiley Papers, Box 1, Folder 12 "Clippings." AAM.

Kiley As a Young Priest (AAM)

His older brother Myles had already decided on a priestly vocation and had been ordained a priest in 1900 for the Archdiocese of Boston. In his late twenties, Moses decided to take the plunge. He was in the parlance of that era a late vocation. With the help and encouragement of his uncle, Father Moses McGarry, C.S.C, and using money he had saved in his working career, he began his philosophy studies at the College of St. Laurent in Montreal where McGarry was the president. McGarry became a guardian angel for his nephew, who demonstrated slightly above average academic skill.[109]

---

109. "Oldest Member of C.S.C. Buried at Notre Dame," July 17, 1936, clipping from *Indiana Catholic*. McGarry remained at St. Laurent until 1904, when he became assistant to the Superior General of the Congregation of the Holy Cross. He moved to the University of Notre Dame where he remained until his death in 1926. "Dr. Moses M'Garry Died in Notre Dame; A Priest 60 Years, clipping from *Chicago Sunday Tribune*, July 12, 1936. His nephew Moses, then Bishop of Trenton, presided at the Requiem Mass at Notre Dame. These materials came from the Archives of the Congregation of the Holy Cross, Notre Dame, Indiana, courtesy of Father Wilson Miscamble, C.S.C.

He graduated in 1906 and entered St. Mary's Seminary in Baltimore. With the help of his Uncle Moses, Archbishop James Quigley of Chicago accepted him as a candidate for the Archdiocese of Chicago and sent him to Rome for his advanced studies. In the fall of 1907, Moses began at the Propaganda University with residence at the North American College. "I am very much pleased to be adopted by Your Grace," he wrote to Quigley, "thus becoming one of your subjects and also to be sent to Rome to complete my studies."[110] He was taller and older than most of his classmates and even some of the faculty. He developed misgivings about this course of study and the long residency in Rome when an academic snafu required that he repeat his philosophy coursework. In protest he wrote to Quigley, "I am thirty years old and have had to pay my own way through college and the seminary thus far. So, I do not think in justice to myself I can afford to spend two years more in philosophy when I have already made two years in the seminary. My average in the senior philosophy class in St. Mary's Seminary Baltimore was 86.5 and 86 and one half for the year's work. This I think should suffice." He insisted on beginning theology, noting that if he had to repeat philosophy, "I should never have come to Rome to begin philosophy."[111] Quigley instructed the school to permit Kiley to begin theological studies. This reluctance to stay in Rome would change.

---

110. Moses Kiley Papers, c. 1911 Madaj Collection, AAC.

111. Moses E. Kiley to James Quigley c. 1907, Madaj Collection AAC.

Kiley (Last Row, Center) as a Seminarian in Italy (AAM)

The Kiley Vision: Purposeful, Legalistic, Duty-Conscious

Despite this initial annoyance, he came to love Rome, especially its ecclesiastical culture. He also developed an ear for Roman gossip. The study of canon law appealed to him and dovetailed with his formal, task-oriented personality. By the end of his studies and approaching priestly ordination in 1911, Kiley wrote to Archbishop Quigley, imploring the archbishop to allow him to remain in Rome after his ordination and finish his studies in canon law. This letter sounded the controlling theme of his life and his approach to priestly and episcopal ministry. "Knowing from my experience of ten years in business and in dealing with people of all classes that the one who knows the most about his business, has the greater success, I concluded that this principle was nonetheless true in the salvation of souls. The people of the present-day wish to know the reasons why. If you are able to tell them why this should be so, and the others not, you will be able to do something.

In a word you will have their confidence and if you lead this way, they will follow…If there is one place more than another that will broaden a man's mind, it is surely Rome and particularly the Propaganda. My conclusion is that at the end of four years you are just about to begin to study intelligently. Before that you are grasping about with vague ideas of everything and knowing little of anything in particular." He remarked in words that would define his approach to priesthood and episcopal leadership, "Canon law is so intimately connected with this that unless you have studied it you will accomplish little. Our professor of Moral Theology…says study your canon law and Moral Theology together and then you will be of some real value in your diocese."[112] The inspiration and guiding light of his ministry were the straight lines of canon law—not scripture, not dogmatic theology, not liturgical life. Everything was spelled out clearly in law. In his personal and professional life, he steadily followed that same vision.

Once again his uncle wrote on his behalf: "The young man wishes to know if your Grace will permit him to spend two extra years in the study of Canon Law. He is very anxious to do so under the new code which will be just about time he will have finished his course of theology in 1911. He wrote to me about the matter as I was the instrument in his being adopted by Your Grace and asked me to let him know if you would grant this permission."[113] Quigley referred the matter to his chancellor Dr. Edward Hoban, who denied the request. "The diocese is in much need of priests at the present that I cannot accede to your request…" Then he made a promise that likely Moses reminded him of: "After years on the mission both you and I will be better able to judge the advisability of your making higher studies."[114] Moses obediently returned to the United States. He had no other option.

---

112. Moses E. Kiley to James Quigley, February 10, 1911, Madaj Collection, AAC.

113. Moses McGarry to James Quigley, September 17, 1909, Madaj Collection, AAC.

114. James Quigley to Moses E. Kiley, March 7, 1911, Madaj Collection, AAC.

The Parish Priest and the Director of Charities

The thirty-five-year-old Kiley was ordained to the priesthood in the Lateran Basilica on June 10, 1911, by Archbishop Giuseppe Ceppetelli, the vicegerent of Rome and titular Patriarch of Constantinople. He had also ordained Angelo Roncalli the future John XXIII, and American Bishops Francis Spellman of New York and John Floersh of Louisville. On August 26, 1911, Kiley was back in Chicago, where Quigley assigned him as a curate at St. Agnes Church on Thirty-ninth and Washtenaw in the Brighton Park neighborhood of the southwest side of Chicago. The church of St. Agnes and its school were anchors in the community, which had significant numbers of eastern European immigrants (Poles and Lithuanians), as well as Italians. The pastor was Father Newton Hitchcock, who was ordained in 1885 in Chicago and like Kiley a delayed or older vocation. Hitchcock was something of a local character—earning himself a slander suit from a Chicago police sergeant whom he denounced from the pulpit at three masses for his unwillingness to contribute to the parish fund.[115] Kiley spent five years with Hitchcock and, in addition to his pastoral duties, he also found time to evaluate articles on marriage for the *Ecclesiastical Review*.[116]

In December 1915, a new archbishop, George Mundelein was appointed to replace Quigley, who had died earlier that year. In 1916 the new archbishop asked Kiley to begin a shelter for homeless men in "Hobohemia"' on West Madison Street in Chicago. The Holy Cross Center for Homeless Men was a six-story former grocery warehouse located on the spot of the Haymarket riots of 1881. Kiley took an active part in rehabilitating the old building. A co-worker later described him as "the padre in overalls" or "the janitor of the archdiocese." Kiley did some of the woodwork and later

---

115. "Priest is Sued for Slander," *Chicago Tribune*, June 2, 1906, p. 5.

116. He often commented on papers by a Franciscan identified as Father Stanislaus. A copy of this article and Kiley's response are in Kiley Papers, Box 2, Folder I, AAM.

personally drove around collecting clothes and soliciting money.[117] The facility was intended to be a half-way house for derelict men and was open to all comers, regardless of race or creed. Other Catholic dioceses—New York, Brooklyn, Philadelphia, and St. Louis—had similar institutions. In addition to sanitary facilities, including a fumigation room, it also had a chapel, individual rooms, and an employment bureau. Men were given tickets to take their meals at nearby restaurants and were expected to seek work. Kiley noted, "We have heard so much about the deserving derelict that we have determined to give him a chance and see what he can make of himself after our healing offices have been administered."[118]

On the upper floors were the headquarters of Central Catholic Charities which had been formed by Mundelein in 1916. The organization was complex, with a lay president and a priest superintendent, but Kiley was the main archdiocesan official in the organization. Here he honed his administrative skills and learned the techniques that Mundelein used to eke money out of parishes and priests, keeping a watchful eye on every penny. After his tenure here he was able to return to Rome.

Roma Aeterna: Returning Home

In 1926, Monsignor Edward Mooney (the future archbishop of Detroit) and the Spiritual Director of the North American College was appointed the apostolic delegate to India. Kiley's classmate Eugene Sebastian Burke, then rector of the college, proposed him as a replacement. In his reports to Chancellor Edward Hoban, Kiley likely reminded Hoban of his earlier "promise" to re-evaluate Kiley's plea to return to Rome. Hoban (a future bishop

---

117. "Named First Director of Vast Catholic Charity Work in Chicago," *Catholic Herald-Citizen*, March 20, 1940, "Clipping File" Box 1, Folder 12, Kiley Papers, AAM.

118. "Catholic Mission Home in Chicago," *The Catholic Columbian* 41 December 15, 1916. n.p.

of Rockford and Cleveland) apparently predicted to Mundelein that Kiley would look for the first opening to escape to Rome. When he was selected to replace Mooney, Mundelein wrote to Hoban: "You called the turn on Moses Kiley's appointment and no doubt he is the happiest man in Chicago. For him to be placed in Rome to absorb the gossip of the world is Moses' idea of earthly paradise and the vista of future possibilities…"[119] Nonetheless Mundelein observed, "…leaving all jobs aside he will be a good addition to the…college and great influence for good with the church."

Mundelein was no sentimentalist. When the archbishop let Kiley go, he not so subtly reminded his subject that Chicago had given him his berth in the clergy and encouraged him while admonishing him to maintain his loyalty to his home See. "We have nobody just now to 'fill your shoes,'" Mundelein wrote. However, he observed, "You have the opportunity of doing splendid work and rendering a great service to the church in this country by helping to mold the spiritual side of these young men away from their homes and families for so long a time and sent to the center of Christendom." In case there was any ambiguity about Mundelein's expectations, the Chicago archbishop made it perfectly clear: "I need not tell you that from time to time when we need your services in Rome for any purpose, I will not hesitate to call on you."[120] Others viewed this promotion as a step up the career ladder. Two years later, Kiley's aging uncle explained to a cousin: "Of course you have heard of the right Rev. Moses. E. Kiley's promotion to the spiritual director of the students at the American College of Rome. The good Lord may yet use him in his church for other things. If success is a sign of divine favor, heaven has put the seal of approbation on all his works since he entered the Holy

---

119. George Mundelein to Edward Hoban, January 31, 1926, Madaj Collection AAC.

120. George Mundelein to Moses E. Kiley, Kiley Papers, January 27, 1926, AAM.

Priesthood."[121] Kiley arrived in Rome on March 26, 1926, and in May 1926, Apostolic Delegate Archbishop Pietro Fumasoni-Biondi formally nominated him to the spiritual director post. He took up residence at *Via dell'Umilta*, where he had been a student.

Kiley conscientiously performed his duties with the young men of the North American College and occupied a post second only to the rector. His preserved talks reflected the consistency of the views he held since his own days as a seminarian. He frequently insisted that the seminarians know the purpose for which they had been sent to Rome and to focus on that as the key to success in the seminary and in their future ministry. His talks were ponderous and didactic, delivered in a sepulchral voice with little warmth. Father Robert McNamara, the best historian of the North American College, characterized Kiley's conferences to the young men as "less brilliant than some which the collegians had heard but nevertheless solid." Philadelphia Cardinal Denis Dougherty expressed it more bluntly: "Kiley is a wretched talker."[122] Kiley occasionally spiced up his talks with homely illustrations drawn from his working-class past, such as how a pulley works. But a more common theme stressed the unworthiness of the individual candidates for the priesthood and the importance of faithful attendance to the duties of their exalted state.

---

121. Moses McGarry to James Doyle, August 1, 1927, Archives of the Congregation of the Holy Cross, Notre Dame.

122. Denis Dougherty to Amleto Cicognani, November 6, 1939. *Chicago: Delegazione Apostolica Negli Stati Uniti, America IV, provista della arcidiocese Liste Episcopale 732 376/39-Morte Cardinal Mundelein,* AVA.

*Kiley (Front Row, Second from the Left)
as Spiritual Director, North American College (AAM)*

If he did wax poetic or sentimental, it was only when speaking of Rome, which he still loved with the ardor of a love-smitten adolescent: "The moment in which one takes his first look at Rome is an epoch in his life. The sight of this city which has exercised such a mighty influence on the world causes his vague notions of ancient history to assume a more distinct form. The classics and historical lessons which he thought so dull in his school days have been endowed with a new life and interest." He continually praised the beauty of the city and extolled the role it has played in the shaping of civilization. The seminarians chosen to go there were exalted beings. "The definite and specific purpose then of your coming to Rome is to better prepare yourselves for the sublime and exalted mission to which it seems God has called you as he called Abraham of old: 'Go forth out of thy country and from among thy kindred and come to the land I shall show you.'"[123] In another talk he declared, "This is what makes a student's life in Rome worthwhile. With intellectual advantages inferior to none of our American centers of learning, there is besides an education of environment and contact, a training of heart and eye and ear, deep and far-reaching in its formative influence and which nowhere else to be attained." He continued, "For the student called to the sacred ministry, his work is done beneath the inspiring glance of Christ's Vicar on Earth and her basilicas and catacombs are shrines as so many open books wherein are written the brightest of the Church's history, perpetual incentives to the noblest thought and deed in emulation of those who have so gloriously gone before us in this divinest of all work, the salvation of souls."[124]

Kiley was not a warm or effusive man but was more like a stereotypical New England Puritan. He had little or no sense of humor and the downside of his years of manual labor made him a workaholic. Yet despite his formal personality and foreboding mien, those who approached him in the

---

123. Kiley Conference, November 15, 1928, Box 2, Folder 4, Kiley Papers, AAM.

124. Kiley Conference n.d, Box 2, Folder 3, Kiley Papers, AAM.

confessional or for direction found him to be gentle and compassionate. On his occasional trips home, he took time to visit the parents of seminarians who could not leave Rome until they were ordained. He was always the first one in the college chapel before morning prayers and Mass—a habit Albert Meyer, his successor, imitated.

In the eight years Kiley spent in Rome, he filled his time with other duties in addition to being spiritual director. Here he sufficiently convinced enough of the right people in the Roman curia that he had leadership potential. At Mundelein's urging, he was chosen to accompany Cardinal Giovanni Bonzano, the papal legate to the Eucharistic Congress of 1926 to be held in Chicago. He accompanied Bonzano across the country with forty-nine other cardinals in a train painted red. It stopped along the way to collect bishops from across the country to attend this major event. He wrote out Bonzano's many talks at various stops and at the Congress itself.[125]

A time-consuming but required task was squiring visitors around Rome—many of them benefactors and some politicians, mostly recommended by Mundelein. Arranging papal audiences, tours of Roman ruins and churches, and meetings with prominent ecclesiastics was a regular part of his typical work week. Countless pictures of him exist sitting or standing grim-faced with these visitors. Likely more satisfying was consulting with different offices or congregations in Rome. Kiley served as the American representative on the Supreme Council for the Propagation of the Faith (an important missionary-funding society that relied quite heavily on American donations).

---

125. Copies of these talks are in the Kiley Papers, AAM. For the Eucharistic Congress, see Kantowicz, *Corporation Sole,* pp. 166-169.

Kiley Escorting Guests in Rome (AAM)

In addition, he was a consultor of the Congregation of the Oriental Church and the Pontifical Commission for Russia. The details of his service and his expertise in these fields are unknown, but he learned very quickly the pathways of power and scooped up large amounts of Roman gossip to repeat to Mundelein, who contacted him frequently. He was discreet, deferential, and his towering height certainly must have convinced his Roman patrons that he possessed *bella figura*.

Perhaps the most satisfying to Kiley with his penchant for Roman gossip were his interactions with the Congregation of the Council. This office oversaw the life of the clergy and received the reports (*relationes*) of all the bishops of the world prior to their *ad limina* visits. Unlike sometimes-anodyne accounts in the Catholic press, these reports often recorded the actual financial status of a diocese, its geographical realities and growth statistics, and discussed the clergy and the diocesan school systems. Kiley pored over these reports and helped explain American conditions to other members of the Congregation. As he later admitted, the Congregation gave him a listening post for all the dioceses of the world. In reports, meetings, and conversations with visiting prelates, he also heard about the Depression-era woes of various American dioceses. One stood out, the Diocese of Trenton, New Jersey, the See of the state capital of the Garden State. Bishops Thomas Walsh and John J. McMahon had previously governed the diocese.

Bishop of Trenton

Trenton would be a challenge, especially since Kiley inherited the debts of one of his predecessors, Bishop Thomas Walsh. Walsh, a priest of the Diocese of Buffalo, was a hard-driving ecclesiastical careerist had who reached the episcopacy a mere eighteen years after his ordination.[126] He served in Trenton from 1918 to 1928. Here, he began a massive building campaign, adding twenty-one new parishes, increasing the number of parochial schools from forty-nine to eighty-nine, and the number of parochial high schools from five to twenty. Most of this was on borrowed money.

In 1928, Walsh departed to become bishop and later archbishop of Newark and handed off the job to another Buffalo priest John J. McMahon. McMahon took office just as the Great Depression was suffocating the economy of the region. He was beset by eye problems and high blood pressure and died at the age of fifty-seven. His maladies were no doubt exacerbated by the heavy burden of debt left behind by Walsh.[127] The See remained vacant

---

126. Regina Waldron Murray, "Third Bishop: Thomas J. Walsh, 1918-1928," in Joseph C. Shenrock (ed.) *Upon This Rock: A New History of the Diocese of Trenton* (Trenton: Diocese of Trenton, 1993), pp. 123-138. James Quigley ordained Walsh.

127. Eugene Rebeck, "Fourth Bishop: John J. McMahon, 1928-1932, in Shenrock, *A New History*, pp. 139-146.

for a year and a half because of this debt. As William J. O'Brien, the head of the Catholic Church Extension Society observed to a financially strapped bishop in California, "You say you are interested in such 'stuff' about others. Well, you can add that the Diocese of Trenton has not been filled in over a year, for the simple reason that forty of its largest parishes down there are bankrupt!"[128]

In early 1934, Kiley was summoned to the presence of Pope Pius XI who informed him that he was to be made a bishop. Two days later, on February 12, 1934, the prefect of the Consistorial Congregation himself, Cardinal Gaetano Bisleti, personally announced Kiley's nomination to the episcopate as bishop of Trenton. This could not have been a surprise to Kiley, who had for years positioned himself for episcopal office. Perhaps he hoped for a more solvent diocese, but he took the plunge in Trenton that had likely been refused by others. He was consecrated in the American church of Santa Susanna in Rome by the Carmelite Cardinal Raffaele Rossi. Archbishop Carlo Salotti of the Propagation of the Faith and Bishop Thomas Walsh served as the co-consecrators. On May 8, 1934, Kiley was enthroned in Trenton's St. Mary's Cathedral by Cardinal Patrick Hayes of New York. He would remain in the Garden State for six long years.

Kiley inherited a diocese of 237 parishes, 301 priests, 100 parochial schools, sixteen high schools, and a Catholic population of 283,968. He also took on a debt of $10 million. While the number of parishes and institutions at risk are unknown, there were clearly enough to make a priest think twice about accepting the diocese. Just as Kiley was starting work on solutions, the Pope established the Dioceses of Patterson and Camden in 1937. The latter broke off six counties from Trenton. The new diocese of Camden

---

128. William O' Brien to Philip Scher, January 31, 1924, Diocese of Fresno-Monterey, Catholic Church Extension Society Papers, Loyola University. O'Brien was an inveterate gossip who had friendly contacts all over the nation because he handed out thousands of dollars from the Catholic Church Extension Society.

had 100,000 Catholics in forty-nine parishes, thirty-one mission churches, thirty parochial schools, and five high schools. It further deprived Trenton of seventy-five diocesan priests and eleven priests of religious communities. Although financial figures are not available, the newly created diocese both helped and hurt Kiley's efforts to bring fiscal stability to Trenton. Some of the parishes and schools that were moved to Camden likely had heavy debt, while others were sources of revenue.

Like Stritch in Milwaukee, Kiley learned the fine art of refinancing and finding other ways to raise revenue for parishes, schools, and Catholic charities. Kiley then began to demonstrate the kinds of administrative skills that had made him successful in Chicago.[129] Working with his chancellor, Father Richard T. Crean, he systematically refinanced a substantial portion of the debt owed by the diocese and parishes, putting the final retirement of the bonds to a much later time. According to one source, he also called on the help of the government's Reconstruction Finance Corporation (RFC), a Hoover-era lending initiative that was continued and expanded by the Roosevelt administration.[130]

In 1940, as he was preparing to leave Trenton, he uncharacteristically bragged about his accomplishments. He thanked the "good Lord and the generous cooperation of the clergy and faithful," for, as he noted, "We have been able during the past five and one-half years, to liquidate a considerable portion of the heavy indebtedness with which the Diocese was burdened and to refinance the balance on very favorable conditions." He reported optimistically, "The long-time loans arranged for from fifteen to twenty years are being reduced to a minimum of five percent annually, and most of these parishes are making even a larger reduction on the principal, some eight to ten percent. The interest on these long-time loans is reduced from six to

---

129. Vincent E. Keane, "Fifth Bishop: Moses E. Kiley, 1934-1940," in Shenrock, *Upon this Rock*, pp. 147-154.

130. Ibid. p. 151.

four percent. The shorter loans for ten years and less are being reduced at the rate of approximately ten percent annually, while the interest on this has been reduced from six to three percent." He concluded, "Whilst the sum total of the indebtedness on all the parishes is still quite large, with the present arrangement it can be carried and liquated without any great difficulty." Kiley leaned on the well-off parishes to contribute to a reserve fund which helped the struggling parishes pay their debts and to provide a nest egg for future parishes or for emergencies.[131]

Kiley's experiences in Trenton locked him into conservative and risk-averse positions regarding diocesan finances. The experience of bank failures led him to place large amounts of cash in bank vaults rather than deposit and secure interest.[132] When he learned that some pastors grew rich by taking all the loose donations from the Sunday collections, Kiley banned the practice in Trenton and later did the same in Milwaukee. All collected monies belonged to the parish.

Just as impressive, Kiley addressed a shortage of clergy: "The Diocese was short about 100 priests when I came to Trenton in 1934, that is there were only about two-thirds as many priests as were needed to care for the spiritual welfare of the faithful." With the loss of priests to Camden, the situation was even worse. Nonetheless he bragged, "I ordained 75 priests for the Diocese since I have been here and there are eight to be ordained this year (1940)." He was proud as well for securing twenty-seven priests for temporary work and increased number of the clergy working with Italian-speaking parishioners from seven to seventeen. He added sixty-six more seminarians and founded a Catholic boy's high school in Trenton.

Kiley kept a low profile in Trenton, commenting once that the local bishop should appear in the papers only twice: the first time when he came to town and the second time when he died. A farewell editorial alluded to his

---

131. Kiley Papers, Box 2 Folder 3 n.d., AAM.

132. Interview with Monsignor Joseph Emmenegger, October 7, 1983, Elm Grove, Wisconsin, AAM.

remote persona: "By reason of a retiring disposition and an intense preoccupation with the spiritual and temporal responsibilities of his office, Bishop Kiley had not become well known to the people of Trenton…he remained aloof from public life, devoting himself exclusively to his exacting duties as a spiritual leader."[133] This no doubt pleased the publicity-shy prelate. His successor, William A. Griffin, brought a new set of priorities to the diocese and enjoyed the financial stability Kiley had brought. Trenton now had 237 churches, 233 diocesan priests, and 100 parochial schools.

The death of Cardinal Mundelein in October 1939 spurred a search for a successor. Apostolic Delegate Archbishop Amleto Cicognani surveyed all the archbishops of the country for their nominations to the Chicago See. Even though the nod went to Stritch, recently opened papers in the Vatican reveal that Kiley was also a strong contender. One of his supporters was recently appointed Archbishop Francis Spellman of New York, whom Kiley knew from his days at the North American College and other encounters in Rome. Spellman thought him an ideal candidate because of his history with Chicago, his work as spiritual director of the American College in Rome "where he was respected and esteemed by the students," his work with Roman congregations, and above all his accomplishments in Trenton as "the serious administrator of a diocese in poor financial condition." Yet Spellman could not resist a backhanded compliment noting sardonically, "He would not be brilliant, but he would be safe."[134]

Kiley was enthroned in Milwaukee on March 17, 1940 (the anniversary of his episcopal consecration). Since St. John's Cathedral was still in ruins, his installation took place in the Church of the Gesu on the campus of Marquette University. Here he offered a rare bit of humor, telling those assembled, "God proposes, man disposes, and the Holy Father sends Moses." But he returned

---

133. Quoted in Keane, *Upon This Rock*, p. 153.

134. Francis Spellman to Amleto Cicognani, October 31, 1929, "Chicago" *Delegazione Apostolic Negli Stati Uniti, America IV, provista della arcidiocese Liste Episcopale 732 376/39-Morte Cardinal Mundelein*, AVA.

quickly to the leitmotiv of his ministerial career: "Of the future, one thing is certain. We will do our duty, for we cannot be altogether faithful to God unless we do our best."[135]

Kiley ruled in Milwaukee from 1940 until his death in April 1953. These were years of war, post-war growth, and rapid institutional expansion of Catholic life. Fortunately for Kiley, much of the hard work of refinancing and dealing with budgetary shortfalls had been done by Stritch. He changed few people in his official family and even managed to get Stritch's old confidant, Roman Atkielski, ordained an auxiliary bishop—along with two of his old colleagues from Rome, Albert G. Meyer who succeeded him, and John Benjamin Grellinger who became an auxiliary in Green Bay. He facilitated the creation of a new diocese in Madison in 1946, which clipped off seven counties of the Archdiocese of Milwaukee. Bishop William P. O'Connor of Superior was appointed as its first bishop.

Rebuilding the Cathedral

This was perhaps the single greatest accomplishment of Kiley's episcopate. Kiley engaged the Brielmaier architectural firm to oversee the rebuilding of St. John's Cathedral. The money came from a heavy assessment on the parishes and continued fund-raising via special collections. In the fall of 1941, Kiley ordered a $500,000 fund drive to finish the cathedral. With the rush of wartime employment and regular salaries, this goal was quickly reached. Kiley tied its rebuilding to the celebration of the centennial of the archdiocese in 1943. Even though William Perry had quit the project in a huff and Father Thomas Plunkett had died, Kiley completed the work, mostly along the lines that Perry and Plunkett had sketched. Since the wooden raftered roof had been destroyed by the fire of 1935, a new iron-girder roof was put in place to assure a more stable and fire-proof structure. Moreover, the footprint of the church

---

135. "Newly Enthroned Archbishop Feted," *Catholic Herald Citizen*, April 6, 1940, p. 1.

was extended sixty-five feet to the south. Work proceeded rapidly throughout 1942, and Milwaukeeans were regularly informed of progress. In September 1942, the cathedral clock was restarted, and the first of the thirteen stained glass windows—one of the cathedral's patron, St. John the Evangelist—done by T.C. Esser Studios was unveiled. Twelve more of the rest of the apostles would follow.[136] Kiley proved to be a demanding micromanager, phoning every day to check on its progress, dropping in unannounced to see that the work was being done properly, and occasionally browbeating the cathedral rector.

Kiley in Front of Newly Installed Window of St. John (AAM)

---

136. To their consternation, the venerable Conrad Schmitt Studio was not given a chance to bid on a contribution to the rebuilding. Conrad Schmitt Studios to Moses E. Kiley, March 10, 1942; Rupert Schmitt to Moses E. Kiley, June 4, 1942, Cathedral File, AAM. A picture of Kiley with the newly installed window of St. John appeared in the *Catholic Herald-Citizen*.

The old cathedral interior had been more ornately decorated and adorned—even as its restrained exterior presented itself to the world. As noted earlier, Stritch and Perry were both taken by the simple elegance of the cathedral tower that had been erected in the 1880s. They wanted the interior of the church to replicate that motif. Kiley agreed. The interior of the new cathedral now more resembled a Roman basilica with a very restrained internal décor. White oak pews were placed, and the seating capacity of the cathedral expanded from 1,000 to 1,400. The cathedral now extended 236 feet, with a width of seventy-six feet and a height of sixty-two feet. The most eye-popping feature was the twin rows of marble columns. Indeed, the new interior was a riot of marble: walls, side altars, statuary. The new sanctuary space was bigger and wider, much more useful for episcopal ceremonies such as ordinations that would resume in the cathedral. Many young men prostrated themselves on the spacious cathedral sanctuary floor while local photographers snapped shots of them from the two sister balconies that overlooked the sanctuary. They would arise to receive the priesthood and the diaconate from the new episcopal throne on the gospel (left) side of the sanctuary, a simple but elegant *cathedra* that remained until the renovations of the twenty-first century.[137]

---

137. A richer description of the restored Cathedral is offered in the centennial history of the church by Harry Bolton, *St. John's Cathedral, 1847-1947* (Archdiocese of Milwaukee, 1947).

Ordinations and New Cathedra in Expanded Sanctuary of St. John's Cathedral (AAM)

Later a new baldachin would be erected over the high altar, held up by eight columns and rising forty feet above the floor. Inside the dome would be the papal crest and a suspended crucifix. Above the carved wood baldachin were the words, *"Hoc facite in meam commemorationem"* (Do ye this in memory of me). Rondelles, reminiscent of the Roman basilica St. Paul-Outside-The-Walls, depicted the Milwaukee archbishops and framed the tier below the roof. The Stations of the Cross, destroyed in the fire, were replaced by Venetian mosaics based on images from St. Anne's Church on Thirty-fifth and Wright. Later, a shrine to the patriarch Moses was also given by the Wisconsin Conference of the Catholic Hospital Association to honor Archbishop Kiley. The cathedral reopened for midnight Mass at Christmas in 1942.

Shrine to Moses, St. John's Cathedral (AAM)

Opening Mass in Cathedral 1942 (AAM)

Renewing the Seminary

The renovation of the seminary buildings also went forward. Curricular changes had already been in the works since 1937, when Stritch laid plans to separate the minor seminary department from the major. The high school and two years of philosophy were transferred to the nearby Pio Nono High School, which had been substantially rebuilt and now enrolled both boarding and day students. Father William Groessel was appointed the rector of the new minor seminary.

In the major seminary building, changes included upgraded sanitary features, new flooring, and the renovation of dining and kitchen facilities. An elevator was installed for those who lived on the upper floors. Paying for all this was a tax on all the diocesan clergy. Here, too, Kiley kept an eagle eye on the project, regularly hectoring the seminary treasurer, Monsignor Nicholas Brust, and occasionally summoning Rector Albert Meyer for tough talk about expenses and the quality of work done. Students of those days recalled how unnerving these meetings were for the reserved Meyer, who sometimes came back to the seminary with puffy eyes from crying or who seemed uncharacteristically rattled by his encounters with Kiley.[138] Kiley also intruded on other seminary practices, including changing Latin textbooks in the middle of the school year, insisting that faculty members sit with students at meals, and making them be present for the annual reading of the seminary rules. Meyer dutifully went along with these demands. With the division of seminary labors, faculties were separated, and a minor and major seminary staff emerged—the former residing at the new minor seminary. A vocation boom began that pushed forward plans for new buildings for the seminaries—both minor and major. In 1949, Kiley erected a new power plant on the seminary grounds as the prelude to the construction of new residences and a theater for the seminarians. The seminary prospered and students avoiding the wartime draft went to school year-round. Kiley ordained scores of Milwaukee priests. The growth of seminary students would hit a peak in an ordination class in 1955 of fifty-six new priests.

Kiley's Long-Suffering Co-Workers

Kiley retained many of Stritch's appointees, including Edmund Goebel who still oversaw the education department. His offices at Fourth and Galena were conveniently away from Kiley's daily supervision. Kiley also retained Monsignor Roman Atkielski, who was promoted to chancellor. In 1947, he was made an auxiliary bishop and moved out from the episcopal residence to the pastorate of the prestigious St. Sebastian Church in Milwaukee.

Kiley brought into archdiocesan service a new cadre of younger priests. One new office was the Confraternity of Christian Doctrine (CCD), promoted by Bishop Edwin Vincent O'Hara, which brought religious education

---

138. Interview with Father Gerald B. Hauser, November 10, 1983.

to children enrolled in public schools—a growing category of young people. He mandated chapters of the CCD in each parish and appointed Old St. Mary's pastor, Monsignor Philip Schwab, as the organizer. Kiley brought into his official family men whom Stritch had selected for higher studies. These included Father Joseph Emmenegger, a native of Monroe, Wisconsin, who was ordained in 1942, and finished his advanced work at the Catholic University of America, studying under the renowned patrologist Johannes Quasten. Another was Father Leo Brust, a native of New Coeln and the nephew of a seminary administrator. He had begun his studies in Switzerland but had to return when war erupted in Europe and finished at the Catholic University of America. He became a fixture in archdiocesan governance for nearly a generation, specializing in property acquisition. He later became an auxiliary bishop. Father (later Monsignor) Sylvester Gass headed the Diocesan Marriage Tribunal and was a respected canon lawyer and one-time president of the prestigious Canon Law Society of America.

Firsthand accounts of Kiley's staff universally recalled him as a hard person for whom to work. He took few vacations and expected co-workers to follow his lead. Apparently, the abstemious Kiley's only indulgence was taking a pinch of snuff each day. Emmenegger acknowledged Kiley's piety and capacity for hard work, but also spoke frankly about his choleric temper, his verbal abuse of underlings, and his occasionally petulant behavior when dealing with archdiocesan priests and seminarians. Emmengger often took the brunt of Kiley's temper. He related one unpleasant experience with Kiley at a priest's funeral, telling the funeral director as they placed the coffin in the hearse that he (Emmenegger) wished that he were in the casket rather than the deceased.[139]

Another Milwaukee priest, who served as a subdeacon at the annual Mass of Chrism on Holy Thursday morning, remembered that on one

---

139. Interview with Monsignor Joseph Emmenegger, October 7, 1983, Elm Grove, Wisconsin, AAM.

occasion that Kiley discovered that the table bearing the holy oils in heavy urns was just a little too far from him. But rather than move his portable faldstool he made the subdeacons pick up the heavy table and move it to him.[140] His special ire was reserved for the editor of the *Catholic Herald-Citizen*, Father Franklyn Kennedy, who, as Blied recalled, "routinely incurred [Kiley's] wrath by attempting to make the *Catholic Herald-Citizen* a dynamic, relevant tabloid."[141] He showered harsh words on the Mother General of the Franciscan Sisters who served in his household when he allowed a rival college to be built on lands where the sisters had hoped to build a hospital.[142]

Yet he could also be tender and sentimental, bursting into tears at the mention of motherhood, which evoked memories of his own mother. He was also kind to priests who drank too much, calling it "the good man's disease" and sending them to the Sacred Heart Sanitarium in Milwaukee, conducted by the School Sisters of St. Francis. Blied wryly observed, "He is reputed to have been a man of great piety, but his stolid demeanor kept [that] from being contagious."[143] In many ways Kiley's years were mostly about finishing what Stritch had planned. Unlike Stritch, however, Kiley micromanaged every step of the building projects, constantly reminding those in charge that they were spending "other people's money."

A New Orphanage

The last big project inherited from the former era was rebuilding of St. Aemillian's Orphanage that had burned down in 1930. By 1950, the temporary facility at Sixtieth and Lloyd needed repair and replacement. But even

---

140. Father Joseph Strenski to author, February 12, 1984.

141. Franzen, Appendix, The Wisconsin Hierarchy, p. a 12.

142. Moses E. Kiley to Mother Bartholomew Frederick, n.d. NAA.

143. Franzen, Appendix, The Wisconsin Hierarchy, p. a 12.

more, the concept of institutional care for dependent children had changed. Childcare advocates rejected large institutions and favored placements in foster homes. Where large institutions continued to exist, professionals urged their subdivision into family-style units where small groups of children could receive more individual care. None of this seemed to affect Kiley, who moved forward to develop a huge new boys' orphanage. Even when state visitors from the Department of Public Welfare's juvenile division and his own director of the orphanage, Father Francis Paulus, urged another direction, Kiley was not open to hearing it. A new director of Catholic Charities, Father Joseph Springob, was easily intimidated by Kiley and offered little resistance to the archbishop's plans. Kiley announced a fund-raising campaign in 1951 led by Frank Surges, who had been Stritch's right hand in the charity campaigns of the 1930s. Surges and others attempted to prepare the way by suggesting that the existing facilities on Sixtieth and Lloyd were fire traps—adding an element or urgency for a new building. Kiley died while the project was underway, but his successor, Albert G. Meyer, dutifully carried out Kiley's wishes. The new orphanage was built and opened in 1956. By the 1960s, the program of St. Aemillian's had shifted from residential care for dependent boys to care and therapy for emotionally disturbed youth. The archdiocese sold this complex in 1989.

War Realities, Parish and School Expansion, and the End of Days

The war years in the Archdiocese of Milwaukee saw restored prosperity as factories and businesses recovered from the Great Depression. With Kiley's permission, Milwaukee sent thirty priests to serve as chaplains in all branches of the armed forces. Those military chaplains came back with harrowing stories of combat, but they also had experienced a flexibility in liturgical practices that they had not known in their years at home. Practices like evening

Mass, celebrating the Eucharist on the hood of a Jeep, giving soldiers general absolution before they went into battle, caring for the wounded, and offering condolences to comrades and families of the slain were among the many experiences of these chaplains. Some made the military a career. Locally, Kiley blessed Gold Star banners, the pennants that hung in the windows of houses where a man was serving, participated in wartime rationing, and blessed popular prayer efforts like the Novena of Our Lady of Sorrows at St. Anthony Church and the Novena to Our Lady of Victory at St. Stanislaus in Milwaukee. The latter was a devotion devised by Milwaukee priest (and later military chaplain) Raymond Punda.

By the late 1940s, the energies required by the rebuilding projects and the toll of his hectoring management style began to affect Kiley. He began to lose weight and moved slower. In 1948, he was so ill that he could not perform the annual ordinations of the priests for the archdiocese. Nonetheless, the demands of pent-up growth would not go away. In the end, although he founded eleven new parishes, this was not nearly enough, and his successor had to create an additional twenty-five. Periodic bouts in the hospital slowed the archbishop, who nonetheless did his duty. He was admitted to St. Mary's Hospital in late 1952 and remained there until his death. The longer he was there, the more he acted like a caged tiger. He even spurned the anointing of the sick offered to him by his former student John Grellinger. Grellinger, who visited him regularly, noted at one point, "He is.... still very gaunt almost like Abraham Lincoln."[144]

Refusing to delegate any authority to his Vicar General Atkielski, he insisted that chancery staffers bring documents, especially those that might be seen by Roman authorities or the Apostolic Delegate, for his inspection and shaky signature. When the hospital chaplain showed up with the

---

144. John B. Grellinger to Albert G. Meyer, February 10, 1953, Meyer Papers, AAC.

Eucharist, Kiley got out of the bed and knelt on the cold hospital floor.[145] While curmudgeonly with his staff, he charmed the nuns and nurses that tended to him—even singing old Irish ballads he remembered from his youth in Nova Scotia. Often, he asked his secretary, "Why am I not getting better?" But his heart was simply wearing out. He died peacefully on April 15, 1953, while his old student Bishop Albert Meyer of Superior recited the prayers for the dying. Later, at the Solemn Requiem at St. John's Cathedral, Meyer would pronounce one of the ritual absolutions over his body. His mortal remains were reposed in an expanded crypt in the cathedral of St. John that he had renovated. By September of that year, Albert Meyer was in that same cathedral receiving the obedience of the clergy as he replaced his former friend and mentor.

---

145. Monsignor Joseph Emmenegger visited Kiley daily in the months he spent in the hospital. Emmenegger interview.

CHAPTER 3

ALBERT GREGORY MEYER (1903–1965)

Archbishop of Milwaukee, 1953 to 1958

A lbert G. Meyer (1903–1965) was the first native son of Milwaukee to become its archbishop. Both sides of his family had Wisconsin roots, immigrating from Germany and settling in Caledonia in Racine County. His father, Peter Meyer (one of ten children), married Mathilda Thelen, the daughter of another Caledonia farmer. Both sides of the Meyer family had reverend uncles—priests of the Archdiocese of Milwaukee. The Meyers moved to Milwaukee, where Peter Meyer opened a grocery store at 179 Warren Avenue. The family welcomed five children: three boys and two girls. Albert, the youngest, was born March 9, 1903.

The German-speaking Meyers were faithful parishioners of Milwaukee's Old St. Mary's Church on Broadway. The family practiced a form of German house religion—praying the rosary together, meal prayers, and regular attendance at Sunday Mass.[146] The two girls of the family became religious sisters. Olivia became Sister Albert Marie of the School Sisters of Notre Dame, and Louise joined the Sisters of St. Agnes. His older brothers

---

146. Interview with Norbert Meyer, October 5, 1983, Milwaukee, Wisconsin, AAM.

went to work after the eighth grade, some of them with their father at the Chain-Belt factory in West Allis, where the family moved.

Meyer with Parents Mathilda and Peter (AAM)

Albert attended the parish school conducted by the School Sisters of Notre Dame and was a frequent altar server at the sisters' motherhouse chapel. When he expressed an interest in the priesthood, the convent assistant chaplain, Father Peter Schnitzler, tutored Albert and his friend James Graham in Latin. However, his hope to enter St. Francis Seminary after the eighth grade was temporarily derailed by the failure of his father's grocery store, which created a crisis in the family finances. Instead, he attended one year (1916–1917) at Marquette Academy. Eventually, with the help and financial support of the Mother Superior of the School Sisters of Notre Dame Convent, Francis Borgia Meek, he was able to enroll at St. Francis Seminary in the fall of 1917. At St. Francis he completed his high school classics coursework.

His classmates remembered him as reserved and even aloof.[147] He had no interest in athletics, nor did he appreciate boisterous or talkative people. He was then and remained to the end of his life an introvert—sometimes giving the impression of being disinterested in other people. Cardinal Alfredo Ottaviani once referred to him as *uomo freddo*. He did, however, have the capacity to make friends with like-minded classmates, including a Lebanese student from Detroit, Joseph Macksood, whom he took home on seminary holidays. He also forged warm, life-long bonds with an equally taciturn young seminarian from Algoma in the Diocese of Green Bay, William Groessel. His superior academic performance and *bella figura* singled him out, and Archbishop Messmer selected him in 1921 to pursue additional studies at the Propaganda University in Rome and reside at the North American College.

Meyer in Rome

Meyer was certainly honored to go to Rome, but he never really rhapsodized about his experiences there as much as his two predecessors. That he was impressed with Rome we know from a few preserved postcards to his parents preserved in his papers in the Archdiocese of Chicago. In these cards, written in the neat cursive script that the Notre Dame Sisters taught him, he described various Roman churches and monuments. He resided in the Eternal City from 1921 until 1930, when he finished his graduate work in Sacred scripture. During those years, Meyer had a front-row seat for a papal funeral (Benedict XV) and a papal election (Pius XI). He witnessed the canonization of Sts. John Vianney and Therese of Lisieux. He also likely attended the 1925 canonization of St. John Eudes whose devotion to the Sacred Heart of Jesus would play an important role in his spiritual life. In the classrooms of Propaganda, he met another generation of Roman teachers—many of

---

147. Interview with Monsignor Anthony Knackert, September 5, 1983, Milwaukee, Wisconsin, AAM. Knackert was a seminary classmate.

whom were still alive and active in church affairs even when he was a bishop and a cardinal. These included future cardinals Ernesto Ruffini, a scripture scholar; Enrico Dante, a specialist in rites and rituals and a papal Master of Ceremonies; Domenico Tardini, a future secretary of state; and Armenian Gregory Agaganian, a popular priest who was actively touted as a successor to Pius XII. Five years into his studies, Monsignor Moses E. Kiley became the spiritual director of the North American College. Because he was such an accomplished student, he advanced to Holy Orders a year ahead of time. In July 1927, he was ordained a priest in the church of Santa Maria Sopra Minerva by Cardinal Basilio Pompilj.

Meyer as Roman Student (ASFS)

After a celebratory trip home (including a visit with his dying sister Olivia), Meyer returned to the Eternal City and finished his seminary coursework, earning a Roman doctorate with a thesis on the indwelling of the Holy Spirit. He began classes at the Pontifical Biblical Institute (the *Biblicum*) and resided at the German College known as the *Anima*. His studies introduced him to biblical languages, especially Hebrew and Aramaic, and brought him under the influence of Father Augustine Bea, S.J., a future cardinal and a confessor to popes. As part of his training, he spent a summer in Palestine doing archaeological work. Through the good offices of Father Marie-Joseph Lagrange, O.P., he became familiar with the main archaeological sites of the Holy Land. He later taught a class in biblical geography at St. Francis Seminary called *From Dan to Beersheba*. His friends also included Bernard Alfrink, a future cardinal from the Netherlands; William Newton of Cleveland, who became one of the founders of the American Catholic Biblical Association; and Rudolf Graber of Eichstatt, Germany, who became the bishop of Regensburg.

Meyer returned to Milwaukee in 1930 just as Messmer was in his final days, and his future was undetermined. Monsignor Traudt assigned him for a year to St. Joseph's Church in Waukesha. Located about twenty miles west of Milwaukee, it was known as a resort town with therapeutic mud baths and access to lakes and rural acreage. St. Joseph's, the only parish in the city, had a busy mass schedule and a large school. Meyer undertook pastoral ministry with seriousness, carefully writing the key points of his sermons on note cards full of lengthy papal quotations. He referred to this year as one of *seelsorge* [pastoral care] and this was really his only sustained exposure to the ministry of a diocesan priest.

In 1931, Meyer was assigned to teach at St. Francis Seminary. He remained on the faculty for sixteen years, where he taught an array of classes in every branch of the seminary program. These included dogmatic and ascetical theology and instruction in Italian, Greek, and Hebrew. In what must have been a disappointment, he was rarely able to teach Sacred Scripture to the seminarians. Since 1918, the elderly and very eccentric New York priest Father Andrew Breen was on the faculty. Breen had been exiled from St. Bernard's Seminary in Rochester after he falsely accused one of his colleagues, Edward Hanna, of Christological heresy.[148] Breen had a reputation as a scripture scholar, having produced the four volume *A Harmonized Exposition the Four Gospels* (1899-1904). Archbishop Sebastian Messmer took him in and appointed him to the St. Francis faculty. He remained there until his death in 1938. By the time Breen died, Meyer was rector and unable to teach classes, and assigned course work to adjunct professor Redemptorist Edward Mangan. Meyer was never a research scholar and did no more than publish a few articles in the seminary magazine *Salesianum*.[149] He participated in the translation of the three Johannine letters for the Confraternity version of the Bible. His classmate William Newton of Cleveland oversaw the project. Meyer's translation and his commentary were included, but he later complained after their publication that the editors had so thoroughly revised his work that he barely recognized it.[150] His students remember him as careful, well-prepared, and unwilling to suffer classroom nonsense. They also observed that his teaching, like his preaching style, was staid and even lifeless.

Meyer served under two rectors, Monsignors Aloysius Muench and Francis Haas. Meyer impressed Stritch, who made him rector in 1937. He

---

148. Richard Gribble, *An Archbishop for the People: The Life of Edward J. Hanna* (New Jersey: Paulist Press, 2006), pp. 36-38.

149. This a sampling of the articles authored by Meyer for the seminary quarterly *Salesianum* "Daniel 9: 24-27 and Its Interpretation of the Seventy Weeks Prophecy," *Salesianum* XXVI. (January 1932): 33-42; "Daniel 9: 24-27 Part II: *Salesianum* XXVII (March 1932): 16-28; "The Revision of the Vulgate," *Salesianum* XXX (January 1935): 10-22; "More than a Prophet," *Salesianum* XXXI (October 1936: 182-188; "The Catholic Biblical Association of America," *Salesianum* XXXIII (July 1938P: 106-110. "You Are My Friends: The Spirit and Practice of Night Adoration in the Home," *Salesianum* XXXIX (July 1944): 91-100.

150. Interviews with Most Reverend John B. Grellinger November 29, 1980, and October 12, 1983, Green Bay, copies in AAM.

commanded respect and inspired the seminarians—especially by imitating Kiley's practice of being the first in the seminary chapel every morning. He was utterly devoted to the seminary, and he rarely left the grounds except to visit his elderly parents in West Allis each Sunday (often with Groessel). He occasionally met with seminary alumni, the vocations-supporting Serra Club, and others at Forty Hours or other spiritual gatherings. These occasions, as all his required moments of socialization, must have been difficult for the introverted Meyer.

He devoted time to managing the seminary, building on the reforms made by Muench, and closely attuning the seminary's practices to the teachings of the Holy See. The 1930s were a time of substantial upgrading of the intellectual life of the seminary system. Pope Pius XI, a former librarian and archivist, had insisted on a reform to seminary education, especially on the graduate level, and with the decree *Deus Scientiarum Dominus* (1931) and the encyclical *Ad Catholicii Sacerdotii* (1935). These two documents provided the framework of the ends and goals of seminary education. Meyer was so taken with the 1935 encyclical that he had words from it inscribed on his tombstone. In 1939, Pius XI had ordered a general visitation of seminaries in the United States and Meyer participated in these along with Archbishop Stritch. There were also plans to upgrade the seminary's physical facilities—long delayed by the failure of fund-raising during the Great Depression.

The Mind of Albert G. Meyer

By the time he was rector, the basic contours of Meyer's mind and personality were fixed. He was deeply affected by what he learned in Rome and developed a profound deference to papal teaching of any kind. His approach to biblical exegesis reflected his unfamiliarity with historical-critical methods of interpretation approved by Pope Pius XII in the 1943 encyclical *Divino Afflante Spiritu* (1943). It was not until Vatican II, and only with the personal assurance of Father Augustine Bea, S.J., the rector of the Biblicum), that he accepted the hermeneutics of historical critical scripture scholarship. At the Council, he and many other bishops were tutored by scholars Augustine Bea, S.J., Barnabas Mary Ahern, C.P., and Francis McCool, S.J., on contemporary biblical studies.

Meyer was more deeply grounded in dogmatic theology and frequently used scripture as a proof text. Like his predecessors, he followed the theology of the manuals, especially Jean Marie Herve's three-volume *Manuale Theologiae Dogmaticae*, which was used at St. Francis for many years. Unlike the philosophical Stritch, who spun webs of theory, or the legalistic Kiley, who took canon law to be his North Star, Meyer found his direction from the words of the Holy Father. No matter how theologically complicated and poorly translated they were for English speakers, Meyer quoted them extensively, especially in public addresses. His devotion had none of the romantic evocations of apologetic church history nor flights of eloquence on the monuments of the Eternal City. Instead, his Roman credentials were summed up in a phrase he used frequently with the seminarians: "*Sentire cum ecclesia*"—literally "to feel with the church." He expected priests to embrace fully the church's teachings, follow its precepts, and obediently respond to the demands of its leaders—especially the pope and the Curia. As an ordination gift to classes, he handed on a small book on the priesthood prepared by Archbishop Amleto Cicognani, the papal delegate to the United States. For Meyer, Cicognani embodied the mind of the Holy Father. Meyer's public discourse was often rich with lengthy and dense papal quotations.

The best example of this was his 1956 pastoral letter, *Decency and Modesty*. When confronted with what commentators called the family crisis after World War II, Catholics made a concerted effort to shore up the traditional view of Catholic marriage: permanent, stable, and open to the procreation of children. Under Kiley and Meyer, a robust Catholic Family Life program was launched as well as the popular Cana Conference, which was imported from the Archdiocese of Chicago. Widespread fears about social trends in the 1950s alarmed Meyer and Catholics: delinquent youth, rock and roll music, going steady, and premarital sex were always on the horizon. Meyer worried about the proliferation of unclean literature, movies, and now television. Absorbing some of the widespread cultural fears of the 1950s, he observed the generation gap that was growing between teens and adults. He included a lengthy section outlining the dangers of keeping company with the divorced. Since the marriage bond was permanent (until dissolved by a church annulment—which was difficult to attain), a Catholic who did this imperiled his or her immortal soul—especially if they married (or attempted to marry) the person. Even if this approach had sometimes difficult pastoral consequences (especially among African Americans), Meyer insisted on it. *Decency and Modesty* was printed and widely distributed throughout the archdiocese and taught in Catholic schools and colleges.

He was fortunate to live at a time when people did not expect their bishops to be glad-handing extroverts. Yet to the consternation of parish priests who hosted him for confirmations, church dedications, or other big events, Meyer's inability to chat or be warm and friendly was a definite liability. One of his co-workers in Superior, Monsignor Alphonse Kress, recalled his discomfort in living in the large episcopal mansion with the taciturn Meyer and especially the silence at the dinner table.[151] In Chicago, he banished the high-living auxiliary Bishop Raymond Hillinger from the episcopal residence because he was too talkative and kept irregular hours, disrupting the order Meyer demanded in the house. Once, during a visit with him in Superior, an official of the Wisconsin State Board of Control observed, "Bishop Meyer is a tall, handsome man, with a fine presence and bearing, and a great deal of dignity." But, she added, "He does not have personal warmth

---

151. Interview with Monsignor Alphonse Kress, September 19,1983, Stetsonville, Wisconsin, AAM.

of Bishop O'Connor [the former bishop of Superior and Madison]. Most of his life has been spent in study and teaching."[152]

Yet, no clergyman feared him as they did Kiley. Nor was there ever any recorded outburst of verbal abuse and humiliation of priests. Although unable to express it in a direct way, his years as a seminary professor taught him to love and respect the priests. "I have always tried to remain close to my clergy," he wrote when leaving the Diocese of Superior.[153] His circle of friends was almost all priests, William Groessel and John Grellinger being two of the closest. Groessel was as quiet and reserved as Meyer. In 1959, the garrulous William Cousins succeeded Meyer. The friendly, back-slapping Cousins was quite a break for Milwaukee priests to have their bishop talk to them and refer to them by their first names.

Meyer was an authentically holy man—perhaps the most devout and deeply pious of all Milwaukee's bishops. Traditional works of spiritual and ascetical theology that he taught to seminarians included *The Spiritual Life* (1930) by Sulpician Adolphe Tanquerey and the collected sayings of Jesuit brother St. Alphonsus Rodriguez. As noted earlier, his fidelity to the seminary schedule of prayer, his pious talks to the seminary Sodality every Sunday night, and his concern for the safety of the tabernacle key (an obsession of his for years) reflected his deep devotion. What he learned as an altar server at Old St. Mary's and from the School from the School Sisters of Notre Dame stayed with him for his entire life.

Yet despite his austere personality, he felt an attraction to a more affective type of spirituality through his devotion to the Sacred Heart of Jesus. This was due in part because of his interactions with Peruvian-born Father Mateo Crawley-Boevey. Edward Crawley-Boevey, born in 1875 in Peru, was nine

---

152. "Report of July 24-25, 1946," "St. Joseph's Orphan Home-Superior, 1942-1946," Wisconsin State Department of Public Welfare: Licensed Child Welfare Agencies, 1915-1964, Wisconsin Historical Society.

153. "Meyer Appointed Archbishop Here," *Milwaukee Journal*, July 28, 1953, p. 1.

when his parents moved to Valparaiso, Chile. His father was English, and he learned the language as a youth. In 1890, he entered the missionary Picpus Fathers (the Congregation of the Sacred Hearts of Jesus and Mary) taking the religious name "Mateo." His health was fragile, and his superiors sent him to live in Europe. He spent years recuperating from serious illnesses and made a special pilgrimage to Paray-le-Monial where the reputed apparitions of Jesus to St. Margaret Mary Alacoque took place. Here he experienced a healing and intensified a deep devotion to the Sacred Heart of Jesus absorbed from his religious community. He believed himself empowered to preach devotion to the Heart of Jesus and was blessed by Pope Pius X and traveled the world as an Apostle of the Sacred Heart. In 1940 he came to the United States. In 1943, Archbishop Stritch of Chicago enlisted him to help celebrate the centenary of the founding of the diocese through a series of lectures at Mundelein Seminary. Stritch's approval was reason enough for Kiley to invite him to Milwaukee, where he moved into St. Francis Seminary for several months.

Father Mateo urged the practice called enthronement and night adoration. This consisted of displaying [enthroning] an image of the Sacred Heart of Jesus in the home and spending a night of prayer before it. Mateo struck a deep chord in both Kiley and Meyer's hearts. On one memorable occasion he thundered at Kiley, "Archbishop, you are an old man!" causing the prelate to weep publicly. Meyer was swept away by Mateo's devotion. He compelled the seminarians to attend his séance-like conferences in the seminary chapel and indulged Mateo's demands for a special diet and a dais and chair for his preaching, which he did sitting down. Mateo often harped on a single word like "obedience" or "faith," which he repeated with ever increasing volume. He closed all his letters to Meyer with the word *Adveniat,* short for *Adveniat Regnum Tuum* (Thy Kingdom Come). Some seminarians were bemused by Meyer's devotion to the tempestuous Mateo (whom he dutifully chauffeured around the archdiocese). Meyer himself later privately admitted to his friend William Groessel that he wished that Mateo's ministry was a bit more theologically grounded and not so emotional.[154] Nonetheless, he truly venerated the man until the preacher's death in 1960. He used Mateo's mantra, *Adveniat Regnum Tuum*, as his episcopal motto.[155]

Meyer had this same feeling for the spirituality of the famed stigmatic Capuchin, Padre Pio of Pietralcina. His contact with this famous spiritual figure came through his cousin, Father Dominic Meyer, also a Capuchin Franciscan who served as Padre Pio's English-speaking secretary. Frequent correspondence between the two men often had Meyer begging the intercession of the famous saint. He implored Padre Pio's prayers when he discovered that he would be chosen to succeed Kiley in 1953. At one point he traveled to Foggia, where Padre Pio lived, to confess his sins. Padre Pio's and Mateo's devotion to the Sacred Heart of Jesus was the common bond that drew Meyer to them.

Superior

In 1946, ecclesiastical boundary shifts in Wisconsin after World War II created a new diocese centered in the state capital of Madison. Portions of the Milwaukee, Green Bay, and La Crosse dioceses were ceded to create the new jurisdiction. O'Connor claimed seniority rights and insisted that he be appointed to start the new diocese. In February 1946, Meyer succeeded him as the seventh bishop of Superior. He was consecrated on April 11, 1946 (ironically his funeral would be on the same day twenty-one years later), and on May 8, 1946, he was enthroned in Superior's Cathedral of Christ the King.

---

154. Interview with William Groessel, October 17, 1983, Milwaukee, Wisconsin, AAM.

155. For additional information about Mateo, consult Marcel Bocquet, SS.CC. *The Firebrand: The Life of Father Mateo Crawley-Boevey, SS.CC* (trans. Francis Larkin) (Washington: Corda Press, 1966). See also Mateo Crawley Boevey, SS.CC., *Father Mateo Speaks to Priests on Priestly Perfection* (trans. Francis Larkin) (Westminster: Newman Press, 1960). Meyer wrote a glowing introduction to this text and praised Mateo's influence on his life.

Meyer's Episcopal Consecration 1946 (AAM)

The Diocese of Superior consisted of sixteen counties of northern Wisconsin that stretched from Minnesota on the west to the upper peninsula of Michigan on the east. It had more than 60,000 Catholics, 149 priests, eighty-six parishes, sixty-one missions, four Catholic high schools, and thirty-two grade schools. The heaviest concentration of Catholics resided in the See city of Superior, which then hosted nine parishes. In addition, two major Native American reservations had long been under the spiritual care of the Franciscan Fathers. Among Superior's clergy was the first ordained Native American priest, Father Philip Gordon.

Superior had for years struggled financially. Its early bishops worked to pay off a huge debt from building a large orphanage and a cathedral. In addition, the diocese had issues with problem priests who had come there from around the country as a sort of *refugium peccatorum*. It was not until 1946 that the diocese finally climbed out of the debt burden. Superior was a definite learning curve for Meyer, who was accustomed to the stability of the seminary regimen. His only real misstep was forbidding young priests from having a car, a common practice in Milwaukee and elsewhere, only to discover that many of these priests needed their autos to go to mission stations. He did all the organizational tasks expected of a bishop of his era: formed a branch of the Diocesan Council of Catholic Women, introduced a newspaper, held clerical conferences (one of which was on the safety of the tabernacle key), and encouraged devotion to the Sacred Heart. For priests, he relied on a mixture of religious orders (Franciscans and Benedictines), but also enjoyed a slight boom in the number of local vocations. By the time he left Superior in 1953, the diocese had fifty seminarians.

However, like his predecessors Meyer found the isolation of Superior emotionally taxing. He experienced bouts of depression that he poured out in long letters to his cousin, Capuchin Father Dominic Meyer. To occupy his time, he re-read papal encyclicals. One document, *Acerbo Nimis* (1905), had directed greater attention to the catechetical instruction of young people and adults. Based on the *Catechism of the Council of Trent*, the pope mandated public instruction on the Apostles Creed, the Ten Commandments, and the Commandments of the Church. Meyer used his down time to work on a series of sermon guides that offered adequate preparation for busy pastors for Sunday sermon. These guides, adopted by Kiley in Milwaukee and by other bishops, were expositions of the theology he learned and taught at the seminary.

To Milwaukee: Bricks and Mortar

In July 1953, he received the news that he had been appointed to succeed Kiley. "I am returning to those who remember me as one of their own."[156] He said farewell to Superior and promised he would seek to have a native son of the diocese replace him. He carried through on this promise and promoted long-serving cathedral rector Monsignor Joseph Annabring as his successor. On September 24, 1953, he was solemnly enthroned in St. John's Cathedral. He spoke for forty-four minutes, carried live by television and radio. "The ties that bind me to the glorious past of the history of the Archdiocese of Milwaukee are many and varied... As seventh in the line which begins with the name of John Martin Henni, in the words of the biblical proverb quoted by Our Lord, 'I have been sent to reap on that which I have not labored...'" The pent-up demands of growth kept him extremely busy for the five years of his Milwaukee episcopate. Before he was done, he substantially expanded the built environment of the Archdiocese of Milwaukee.

The archdiocese grew from 457,397 to 567,440 during the years of Meyer's episcopate. Catholic numbers spiked so rapidly around the state that Meyer and the other Wisconsin bishops launched a massive census called *Operation Doorbell*, where lay canvassers were engaged to meet and count all the Catholics in their respective dioceses. Kiley had foreseen this growth, and he wrote to the priests in September 1943: "A recent survey of the archdiocese reveals that when this devastating war comes to an end...many new parishes will have to be established." Kiley attempted to raise a fund of $100,000 to lend to new parishes. He also entrusted the survey for new parish sites to Monsignor Leo Brust, who became chancellor in 1946. Brust was put in charge of acquiring land for the archdiocese. He followed studies from the telephone company, shopping-center expansion, local municipal government, and the Southeastern Wisconsin Planning Commission. He

---

156. "Meyer Appointed Archbishop Here," *Milwaukee Journal*, Julu 28, 1953, p. 1.

recalled, "doing lots and lots of riding many, many miles driving around the diocese…consulting local priests. We would determine locations especially with the help of local pastors where a parish ought to go."[157] He carefully followed the plans of home builders and the extension of utility lines (gas and electricity) into the expanding areas, especially around the Milwaukee metropolitan area.[158] Milwaukee County saw an increase of 18.9 percent in its Catholic population. But most of this growth occurred in the suburbs. Catholic numbers in Waukesha, Ozaukee, Washington, Racine, Kenosha, and Fond du Lac counties also began to burgeon. Meyer ended up approving the creation of seventeen new parishes and the raising of six missions to full-time parish status. The post-war years were the longest single period of expansion in the history of the archdiocese.[159] In early 1956, he wrote to Father Joseph Emmengger, now in Rome, "Milwaukee continues to boom and the problems of procuring new parish site continues to occupy a lot of attention. The building activity seems to be without end!"[160] In the 1950s, the old urban neighborhoods of the city declined as racial succession and freeway building altered the demographics of the city. The changing conditions of urban Catholic life would be a concern for his successors.

Schools, too, began to burst at the seams, with Catholic grade school students increasing from 62,136 to 88,599. In one year alone, the number of students under Catholic instruction rose by more than 8500 students. Meyer

---

157. Interview with Most Reverend Leo J. Brust, December 16, 1983, Milwaukee, Wisconsin, AAM.

158. Moses E. Kiley to "Reverend and Dear Father," September 29, 1943, Kiley Circular Letters, Box 2, Folder Six, AAM. Interview of Most Reverend Leo J. Brust, December 16, 1983, Milwaukee Wisconsin, AAM.

159. "Founded 22 New Parishes in the Archdiocese," *Catholic Herald-Citizen*, November 15, 1958, p. 1.

160. Albert G. Meyer to Joseph Emmenegger, February 16, 1956, Meyer Papers, Archives of the Archdiocese of Chicago (AAC).

approved the building of seventy-four new grade schools and twenty-two additions to existing school buildings. Consolidation and new building shrunk the number of high school buildings, but the number of secondary school students increased from 9,653 to 12,610 between 1953 and 1958.

The case of St. Aemillian's was still on the agenda, as the fund drive begun by Kiley now amassed enough to begin planning a building. The firm of Brust and Brust drew up plans for a huge new orphanage. Meyer now had to confront the reality that for nearly a generation, childcare experts and some diocesan officials considered these large institutional facilities outdated and even counterproductive. The Director of Charities Monsignor Joseph Springob and Father Joseph Emmenegger urged Meyer to consider creating three small cottages instead of the big institution that had been planned. But after meeting with the Archdiocesan Consultors—a group of senior priests, many of whom Kiley had appointed—he received contrary advice.[161] They urged him to follow through on the plan Kiley had advanced and for which funds had been raised. Always deferential to senior clergy, Meyer broke ground for the new facility in 1954 and dedicated it in 1956.[162] By 1962 it had become a residential center for troubled adolescents. Despite the good will of the staff and sisters who worked there, the building soon became a white elephant that the archdiocese sold in 1989.[163]

A vocation boom transformed the archdiocesan seminary. In 1953 the archdiocese had 655 seminarians in the major and minor seminaries. By 1958 there were 693 seminarians—most of them for Milwaukee, but also for

---

161. Interview with Monsignor Joseph Emmenegger, October 17, 1983, Elm Grove, Wisconsin. Interview with Most Rev. Leo J. Brust, December 16, 1983, Milwaukee, Wisconsin, AAM.

162. "Bless New St. Aemillian Home on October 2," *Catholic Herald Citizen* September 22, 1956, p. 1.

163. Frank Bleidorn, "A Slice of History, Beginning of St. Aemillian Home," *Salesianum* (Summer 2000): 29-36.

other dioceses in Wisconsin and elsewhere. The need for space to welcome the men pressed hard. Even though the major seminary had tried to cap the enrollment at 280 in 1953, more men sought entrance. Meyer went forward with the expansion plans. Brust and Brust provided blueprints for a new dining hall, an expanded auditorium, and a much-needed residence hall with a new modernistic chapel. In 1954, he launched a Seminary–Charities fund drive and broke ground for the $3 million addition in January 1955. This new complex of buildings was formally dedicated on September 11, 1956, the official celebration of the seminary's centenary. Meyer welcomed back former professors and rectors; Bishop William P. O'Connor of Madison; Archbishop Aloysius Muench, then Apostolic Nuncio to Germany; and other Wisconsin bishops. The preacher of the day was Cardinal Stritch.[164] The new Heiss Hall welcomed the overflow of seminarians. As the number of seminarians shrank in the 1980s, this structure eventually was given over to the use of the Franciscan Sisters. It was razed in 2024, leaving only the magnificent mosaic of the old chapel standing as an outdoor shrine. The pace of Milwaukee's building and the demands for episcopal ministry were unsettling to Meyer, who suffered a slight nervous collapse, which he attributed to an ulcer.

In his years in Milwaukee Meyer was a conservative leader, hewing closely to the example of both Stritch and Kiley. He took the same hands-off policy when called to facilitate an end to a bitter strike in Kohler—even though it polarized the Catholic community of Sheboygan for years. When local priests wanted to preach a sermon on the topic, he refused them permission.[165] The strike, the second since the 1930s, began in 1954 and lasted until the 1960s. However, Meyer did permit a local priest, Father John Carroll,

---

164. "Break Ground for First of New St. Francis Seminary Buildings," *Catholic Herald Citizen* January 29, 1955, p. 1; "Directed Expansion of the Major Seminary," *Catholic Herald Citizen,* November 15, 1958, p. 5. See also Gabriel Ward Hafford, "The Building Program," *Salesianum* 51 (October 1956): 173-178.

165. Father John Carroll to Sheboygan Priests, September 26, 1955. Carroll File, AAM.

pastor of St. Clement's Church in Sheboygan, to attempt mediation. Later, he even quietly encouraged the efforts of National Catholic Welfare Conference emissary Sulpician Father John Cronin, assistant director of the Social Action Department), to bring an end to the strike. All this was to no avail. When publicity about the backroom Catholic efforts to settle the strike leaked out, Meyer wrote privately to the head of the Kohler Company, "May I assure you that even though we were aware of these conversations, none of this premature publicity came from our office...I have followed with deep concern the events that have led up to these conversations..." [166] Despite his concern, he never spoke publicly on those issues.

Meyer also kept his distance from the Specialized Catholic Action Movements that had grown in the late 1940s. Father John Russell Beix and his dedicated followers at the Cardijn Center continued their leadership of the numerous cells of the YCS and the YCW. Beix died in 1952, and the leadership of the movement passed to Father Eugene Bleidorn. A former student of Meyer, Bleidorn was anxious to allay Kiley's fears about these movements. He pleaded with Meyer to visit the center. The archbishop agreed to this on two occasions but insisted that no pictures be taken while he was there.[167] Nonetheless, he did speak encouragingly to the workers and appointed Bleidorn a full-time chaplain, relieving him from teaching duties at the minor seminary.

In January 1958, the mysterious end of Stritch's tenure in Chicago had begun. The aging Cardinal had received a missive from the Apostolic Delegate appointing him the Pro-Prefect of the Congregation of Propaganda

---

166. Albert Meyer to Walter Kohler, February 17, 1957, Meyer Papers, AAC.

167. Meyer visited the Cardijn Center on January 15, 1954, and November 1, 1956. Cardijn Center Papers, Box 1, Board of Directors Meeting Minutes, January 13, 1954. See also Cardijn Center Newsletter, November 1956, Cardijn Center File, AAM. Interview with Eugene Bleidorn, November 5, 1983, Milwaukee, Wisconsin, AAM.

in Rome. Stritch was ordered to leave Chicago and move to the Eternal City to assume his new duties. Although he begged to be relieved of the appointment, he dutifully went to Rome in late April 1958. There his health deteriorated badly, and he had to have his right arm amputated. By May 27, 1958, he was dead. Chicago needed a new bishop, and the archbishop of Milwaukee was selected. Meyer did not want to go, lamenting later that he would be buried in a "cold Chicago mausoleum" instead of the St. Francis Seminary Cemetery he loved so much.[168] His years as the Archbishop of Milwaukee had been brief, but eventful. His tenure in Chicago would be equally brief, with long absences at the Second Vatican Council and his premature death in 1965 of a brain tumor. Stritch, Kiley, and Meyer would still live in the glow of pre-conciliar Roman Catholicism. But a new Milwaukee Catholicism was about to emerge that would confront yet another Chicago bishop, William Edward Cousins.

---

168. Interview with Most Reverend Cletus F. O'Donnell, September 12, 1983, Madison, Wisconsin, AAM.

Meyer Arriving in Chicago with Msgr. George Casey (AAM)

CONCLUSION

Four more archbishops would come to Milwaukee after Stritch, Kiley, and Meyer: William E. Cousins (1958-1978); Rembert G. Weakland, O.S.B.; (1978-2002); Timothy M. Dolan (2002-2009); and Jerome E. Listecki (2009-2024). As I write this, we are awaiting the name of the man who will be the tenth in a line extending back to John Martin Henni. A future historian will have the joy of making sense of the impact of these men on the life and culture of the Archdiocese of Milwaukee. All of this will have to be done within the context of the tremendous changes in Catholic life wrought by Vatican II and its aftermath, as well as the significant social, political, and cultural transformations in the world and America that stretched from the 1960s to the present day. As all authentic historical writing, it will be a challenging and complex task. Samuel A. Stritch, Moses E. Kiley, and Albert G. Meyer were shaped by the intellectual dominance of Neo-Scholasticism given in their Roman seminary formation. Their lives attest to the powerful and compelling influence of this ideology on the leaders of local churches. In their official capacity, all of them drew from the structured, orderly, and clear principles enunciated in Roman manuals and reinforced by the highest authority in the Church. Deferential to Roman authority, compelled by a legalistic view of their duties and responsibilities (especially defined by the 1918 Code of Canon Law), and existing in a sphere of clarity about their role and responsibility, they provided authoritative and mostly good leadership to the Milwaukee archdiocese. Priests generally respected them—and in the case of Kiley, may have been afraid of him. They were consequential figures in the shaping of the local church. Their lives and work are a good window into an important era of U.S. Catholic history. It also offers a departing point for a long-overdue examination of the impact of Roman education on American clergy.

But apart from their offices and official dicta, what can we say about them as people? Samuel Stritch was perhaps the most likeable and popular of them all. Despite his sometimes-confusing flights of intellectual fancy and his dilatory ways, he had a warmth and kindliness about him that wore well on people. His penchant for assigning the unpleasant tasks of his job (e.g., clerical discipline) to members of his staff burnished his benign reputation. No one knows what his struggle with depression did to his perceptions of others. He needed to rest frequently and spent as much time as he could afford in warmer climates (Florida and Tennessee). He could be frank on some issues, but in the end, as his priests in Chicago frequently characterized him, he was "tolerant." His positions on race could best be described as paternalistic—although he kept close to him Father Plunkett, who was a true apostle to African Americans and admired and financially supported the work of Milwaukee Capuchins who labored among the city's Black population. In only a few instances did he ever use the N word in his preserved correspondence. The volume of letters from Toledo and Milwaukee folks in the largest collection of his papers in Chicago suggest that he left a positive impression wherever he went.

Moses Kiley was another story. He was administratively competent, and for his successful rebuilding of the Cathedral of St. John the Evangelist alone he deserves the place of honor in the rondelles along the walls of that church. What we know about him comes only indirectly from his own sources—preserved letters and talks in the archives of the Archdioceses of Chicago and Milwaukee. We know little about his reception in Trenton, since most of the papers of his era were destroyed in a fire. Externally, it seemed like a great success—and managing church finances during the Great Depression certainly merited any prelate a respite from time in Purgatory. But, according to those who knew him and would speak honestly, he had personal dysfunctions that worked to the detriment of the church—especially his ministry to priests. He could be cold and verbally abusive, and he micromanaged affairs to the distraction of good and capable men whom he placed in charge of archdiocesan institutions. As he grew older and sicker, he became more choleric. Even his "beloved sons," John Grellinger and Albert Meyer, both suffered his wrath. Working with the petulance of mercurial bishops was "part of the package" of those days (viz. William Henry O'Connell of Boston), but even within that historical framework, yelling at adults or demanding unending work was unacceptable. He sometimes treated priests like children. He seemed to have no lay friends and just a few family who kept up with him. To his credit, he had capable subordinates, but many priests feared him and were glad to stay away from him.

Albert Meyer enjoyed more respect and kept up with the breakneck growth of the archdiocese. The deference accorded him came of course from his office, but also from his years as rector of St. Francis Seminary. Future priests noted his exceptional piety and fair-mindedness. No one doubted his essential holiness (perhaps his most significant trait) and his very presence evinced respect. There is no record of him verbally abusing anyone. What hampered his effectiveness was his introverted nature. He could not make small talk or engage on a personal level with the thousands of people he met. But where his kind nature is best revealed is in his personal correspondence, which always contained fragments of memories, affectionate words, and heartfelt offers of prayer and condolences. Meyer also revealed the limits of his intellectual formation. Although trained in scripture, he could not conceive of the text as anything other than a valid proof-text for the truth of the Catholic faith. When he arrived in Chicago, he found priests who were studying new forms of scriptural exegesis at the Maryknoll Seminary in Glen Ellyn. He was alarmed, especially when he received letters from disgruntled priests accusing the presenters of heresy. However, he probed the situation with his old teacher in Rome, Father Augustine Bea S.J., the confessor of popes. When Bea assured Meyer that these methods had the approval of church hierarchy, he accepted them and became a more active participant in the debates of Vatican II. It was the kindly and non-threatening Passionist scripture scholar Barnabas Mary Ahern who gently tutored him and other bishops in these methods. But being who he was, he could not accept these things unless they had the sanction of high church officials. He died in April 1965, before the sometimes-tumultuous aftermath of Vatican II reshaped the U.S. Church. Of course, too, it must be said in the aftermath of recent history, all of them failed to manage the crisis of clerical sex abuse. These failures would come back to haunt the Milwaukee church.

Each of their tenures surfaced issues that would later become important in the years after their terms ended. For Stritch, the uneasy relationship between public and private charity was a challenge of his years. The Great Depression changed many things in American life—but none so profoundly as the need for a strong social safety net for Americans who, through no fault of their own, experienced poverty, homelessness, and dislocation. Industries that had fueled the relative prosperity of the region and on which the church relied for voluntary donations fell radically short. Private institutions and even local outlets of relief were exhausted, and the federal government had to step in to provide funds, jobs, and help. From this time forward, public and private social welfare would have to work out a new covenant of cooperation. Catholics still fund their own charities—many of which are quite effective. But they alone cannot deal with the problems generated by economic collapse on the scale of the Great Depression or even less severe downturns. Stritch and other Catholic leaders were disconcerted that dependent childcare, education at every level, and overall concern for the common good increasingly became a function of the state. Kiley's challenge was learning how to function in a modern economy where banks and other institutions were necessary to underwrite debt. His conservative fiscal policies (e.g., keeping cash in bank vaults) likely cost the archdiocese thousands of dollars in interest.

Meyer took his time breaking out of the intellectual milieu of his seminary years. However, the world of 1950s Milwaukee was changing rapidly. The city itself and its environs were being reshaped by the advent of the interstate system—the network of roads that would bring significant demographic change to the archdiocese. The implications of the shift of the vital center of the diocese to its extremities was scarcely understood by anyone. Likewise, as the growth of the city's African-American community was exploding in the 1950s, there were only a few priests and religious in the city who noted it. The practical solution to the race problem—as it was called at the time—was the conversion techniques used so effectively by the Capuchin Fathers and the Racine Dominican Sisters at St. Benedict the Moor in Milwaukee. Only a generous layman, Harry John, heir to the Miller Brewing fortune, met the challenge with outreach to African-American youth—aided by seminarians like young James Groppi, among others.

It is impossible to pigeonhole these prelates as either good or bad or expect them to be aware of issues that would only surface after they were gone. Stritch did much good, but he also could be pessimistic and gloomy about cultural change. Kiley was a good builder and organizer, but his sometimes tyrannical and heavy handed ways created an atmosphere of fear among those whose good will he needed. Meyer was authentically holy and kind, but his introverted ways, embarrassing silences, and poor speaking abilities did not help him. Like the biblical characters of old—David, Solomon, Peter, and Paul—they were a mixture of darkness and light. So were their successors.

INDEX

A

Acerbo Nimis (1905) 118
Ad Catholicii Sacerdotii (1935) 111
ad limina 51, 88
Adveniat Regnum Tuum 115, 116
African Americans 14, 15, 24, 32, 37, 38, 113, 128, 131
Agaganian, Gregory Cardinal 108
A Harmonized Exposition the Four Gospels 110
Ahern, Barnabas Mary C.P. 112
Alacoque, St. Margaret Mary 115
Alfrink, Bernard Cardinal 109
Algoma (Wisconsin) 107
Alter, Karl J. Archbishop 31, 35
Alverno College 60
American Catholic Biblical Association 109
Anima 109
Apostle of the Sacred Heart 115
Apostolate of Suffering 38
Apostolic Delegation 25
Archbishop's Emergency Charity Campaign 48
Archbishop's Fund Appeal 46
Archdiocesan Consultors 121
Arkansas
    Pine Bluff 15
Atkielski, Roman R. 53, 56, 94, 99, 103
Augustinians 58

B

Baddeck (Nova Scotia) 76
Ballyheigue (Ireland) 11
Barbian, Joseph 37, 52, 55, 58, 60
Baron, Rabbi Joseph 72
Bea, Augustine, S.J. 109, 112, 130
Beix, John Russell 66, 123
Benedict XV, Pope 107
Bergan, Gerald 20
Bergen, Ralph 53
Bertram, Adolf J. Cardinal 70
Bisleti, Gaetano Cardinal 90
Blatz, Valentine 47
Bleidorn, Eugene 123
Blied, Benjamin 3, 4, 5, 8, 12, 21, 22, 40, 52, 101
Bolivia 55
Bonzano, Giovanni Cardinal 87
Boston, Archdiocese of 20, 77, 129
Boston Transit Lines 76
Breen, Andrew 110
Breig, Augustine C. 40
Breslau, Diocese of 70
Brielmaier Firm 94
Brighton Park (Chicago) 81
Brinkmeyer, Henry 16
Brooklyn, Diocese of 82
Brothers of the Holy Cross 50
Bruce, Frank 47
Bruce, William George 65
Brust and Brust 121, 122
Brust, Leo J. 100, 119

Brust, Nicholas...98
Buerhle, Marie Cecile.....................................19
Buffalo, Diocese of...89
Burke, Eugene Sebastian...............................82
Byrne, Thomas Sebastian Bishop 13, 14, 15, 24, 26, 28

C

Caledonia (Wisconsin)........................60, 105
Camden, Diocese of.........................90, 91, 92
camerata (cam)..19
Cana Conference..112
Canon Law Society of America 100
Cape Breton Island...76
Capuchins.........................116, 118, 128, 131
Cardijn Center..66, 123
Cardijn, Joseph 66
Cardinal Stritch College/St. Clare 60
Carroll, John...122
Catechism of the Council of Trent............118
Cathedral Chapel (Toledo)..........................34
Cathedral of Christ the King
 (Superior)..116
Cathedral of Our Lady Queen of the
 Most Holy Rosary (Toledo) 34, 36
Cathedral of St. Francis de Sales
 (Toledo) 34
Cathedral of St. John the Evangelist...7, 43, 45, 46, 73, 93, 94, 95, 97, 98, 104, 119, 128
Cathedral of St. Mary (Trenton)...............90
Cathedral of the Incarnation (Nashville)26
Cathedral of Toledo, Spain..........................34
Catholic Action.6, 62, 63, 64, 65, 66, 67, 68
Catholic Charities (Milwaukee)........50, 102
Catholic Charities (Toledo).........................31
Catholic Church Extension Society 90
Catholic Family Life.....................................112
Catholic Herald-Citizen.............................101
Catholic Hospital Association 97
Catholic Social Welfare Bureau 40

Catholic University of America.......60, 100
Catholic Youth Organizations (CYO).....65
Central Catholic Charities (Chicago) 53, 82
Ceppetelli, Giuseppe Cardinal.................81
Chain-Belt 106
Chicago, Archdiocese of..... 6, 9, 15, 17, 20, 22, 37, 40, 53, 73, 75, 78, 81, 83, 91, 93, 107, 112, 113, 115, 123, 124, 128, 129
Chicago, City of ...15, 34, 65, 66, 81, 83, 87, 125
Christian Brothers..26
Christian Brothers College........................26
Cicognani, Amleto Archbishop 57, 93, 112
Cincinnati, Archdiocese of... 13, 15, 16, 28, 67
Cincinnati, City of...15
Clarke, John..65
Cleveland, Diocese of...17, 28, 83, 109, 110
Code of Canon Law...................... 5, 31, 127
College of St. Laurent.................................77
Comes, John T...34
Community Chest..50
Confraternity Bible....................................110
Confraternity of Christian Doctrine
 (CCD)..99, 100
Congregation of Propaganda.................123
Congregation of the Council 88
Congregation of the Holy Cross..............76
Congregation of the Oriental Church.....88
Congregation of the Sacred Hearts of
 Jesus and Mary (Picpus Fathers).......115
Consistorial Congregation 90
Coughlin, Charles E.....................................68
County Cavan (Ireland).............................15
County Kerry (Ireland)..............................11
Cousins, William Archbishop...... 114, 124, 127
Crawley-Boevey, Mateo SS.CC.... 114, 115, 116
Crean, Richard T...91
Cronin, John S.S. 123

INDEX

Crump, E.H. "Boss" 25
Cruse, Timothy Messer 29
Czernoch, John Cardinal 34

D

Dante, Enrico Cardinal 108
Decency and Modesty 112, 113
del Val, Rafael Merry Cardinal 19
Detroit, Archdiocese of 67, 68, 82, 107
Deus Scientiarum Dominus (1931) 111
Diocesan Council of Catholic Women
   (Superior) 118
Divino Afflante Spiritu (1943) 111
Dohn, Leo 65
Dolan, Timothy M. Cardinal 127
Dominican College 60
Dominican Order 64
Dominican Sisters of St. Cecilia 12
Dorcas Chapel 5
Dougherty, Denis Cardinal 84
Downer College Normal School 58

E

Ecclesiastical Review 81
Eichstatt, Diocese of 109
Ellis, John Tracy 9
Emergency War Relief 35
Emmenegger, Joseph 100, 120, 121
Enlightenment 24
Ethnic Diversity 31
      French-Canadian 31
      German 12, 31, 56, 71, 72
      Hungarian 31, 34
      Irish 6, 12, 27, 31, 56
      Italian 31, 56, 57, 58, 81, 92
      Lithuanian 81
      Mexican 31
      Polish 31, 56, 81
Eucharistic Congress (Chicago) 34, 87
Eudes, St. John 107

F

Fargo, Diocese of 44
Farrelly, John Patrick Bishop 17, 18, 28
Floersh, John A. Archbishop 25, 81
Foggia 116
Fond du Lac, City of 4, 5, 39, 60
Fond du Lac County 120
Frederick, Sister Bartholomew O.S.F. 59
From Dan to Beersheba 109
Fumasoni-Biondi, Pietro Archbishop.... 40, 84

G

Garden State (New Jersey) 89, 90
Gass, Sylvester 22, 100
Gesu Church 64, 65, 73, 93
Gleason, Neil 42
Gleason, Philip 21
Goebel, Edmund 60, 64, 99
Goldsmith Building 41
Gordon, Philip 117
Graber, Rudolph Bishop 109
Grace, William, S.J. 59
Graham, James 106
Great Depression 6, 7, 35, 50, 57, 69, 89, 102, 111, 129, 130
Great Falls, Diocese of 68
Green Bay, Diocese of 94, 107, 116
Grellinger, John Benjamin Bishop 94, 103, 114, 129
Griffin, William A. Bishop 93
Groessel, William 98, 107, 111, 114, 115
Groppi, James 131

H

Haas, Francis Bishop 47, 67, 110
Hackett, Anna Mae 63
Hackett, Hoff, and Thiermann 41
Hanlon, James 4
Hanna, Edward Archbishop 110

Harvard University 3
Hayes, Patrick Cardinal 90
Haymarket riots 81
Heiss Hall 122
Heiss, Michael Archbishop 3
Henni, John Martin Archbishop 45, 119, 127
Herve, Jean Marie 112
Hillinger, Raymond Bishop 113
History of the Catholic Church in Wisconsin 5
Hitchcock, Newton 81
Hitler, Adolf 69, 71, 73
Hoban, Edward Bishop 80, 82, 83
Hobohemia 81
Holy Cross Cemetery 56
Holy Cross Center for Homeless Men 81
Holy Name Society 42, 48, 64, 65, 73
Holy Rosary of Pompeii (Kenosha) 56, 57, 58

I

Indiana 12
Innitzer, Theodore Cardinal 71
Ireland 11, 15

J

Janesville, City of 39
Janiculum Hill 20
Jews 32, 70, 71, 72
John, Harry 131
Johnsburg (Wisconsin) 3
Johnson, George 32, 33
Johnson, Peter Leo 4
John XXIII, Pope 81

K

Katzer, Frederick X Archbishop 3, 4
Kennedy, Franklyn 101
Kennedy, Thomas 17, 20

Kenosha, City of 39, 42, 56, 57, 65
Kenosha County 120
Kiley, John 76
Kiley, Margaret McGarry 76
Kiley, Mary 76
Kiley, Moses E. Archbishop 5, 6, 7, 10, 20, 23, 27, 50, 73, 75, 76, 77, 78, 79, 80, 81, 82, 83, 84, 85, 86, 87, 88, 89, 90, 91, 92, 93, 94, 95, 96, 97, 98, 99, 100, 101, 102, 103, 104, 108, 111, 112, 114, 115, 116, 118, 119, 121, 122, 123, 124, 127, 128, 130, 131
Kiley, Myles 77
Knights of Columbus 48, 63, 65
Kohler, City of 122
Kohler Company 69, 123
Kress, Alphonse 113
Kristallnacht 72
Ku Klux Klan (KKK) 32

L

La Crosse, Diocese of 116
Lagrange Marie-Joseph, O.P. 109
Lake Nagawicka 64
Lateran Basilica 24, 81
Lateran Treaties of 1929 69
Leo House 70
Leo XIII, Pope 9, 67
Lepicier, Alexis O.S.M. Cardinal 22
Lewis, Eugene 11
Lisieux, St. Therese 107
Listecki, Jerome E. Archbishop 127
Little Rock, Diocese of 14
Louisville, Archdiocese of 25, 81

M

Macelwane, Francis J. 33
Macksood, Joseph 107
Madison, City of 3, 39
Madison, Diocese of 94, 114, 116, 122
Makowski, Anthony 56

INDEX

137

Mangan, Edward C.Ss.R, ... 110
Manuale Theologiae Dogmaticae 112
Margaree (Nova Scotia) 76
Marian College/University 4, 5, 60
Marquette Academy 106
Marquette Stadium 73
Marquette University 4, 59, 64, 93
Marshall and Ilsely Bank 41
Mary Manse College 33
McCool, Francis S.J. 112
McGarry, Moses C.S.C. 76, 77, 83
McMahon, John J. Bishop 89
McNamara, Robert 84
McNicholas, John T. O.P. Archbishop 67
McWilliams, B.F. 36
Meek, Mother Francis Borgia S.S.N.D. .. 106
Memphis, City of 15, 24, 25, 26, 27, 29
Merten, Sister Letitia O.S.F. 59
Messmer High School 43, 49, 60
Messmer, Sebastian G. Archbishop 3, 36, 40, 43, 47, 48, 55, 56, 63, 107, 109, 110
Meyer, Albert G. Archbishop 5, 7, 10, 87, 94, 98, 99, 102, 104, 105, 106, 107, 108, 109, 110, 111, 112, 113, 114, 115, 116, 117, 118, 119, 120, 121, 122, 123, 124, 125, 127, 129, 130, 131
Meyer, Dominic OFM. Cap. 116, 118
Meyer, George 53
Meyer, Mathilda Thelen 105, 106
Meyer, Olivia (Sister Albert Marie S.S.N.D. 105
Meyer, Peter 105, 106
Meyer, Sister Louise C.S.A. 105
Michigan 55, 117
    Royal Oak 68
Miller Brewing 131
Milwaukee Archdiocesan Council of Catholic Women (MACCW) 63
Milwaukee, Archdiocese of 3, 5, 6, 7, 9, 10, 15, 23, 35, 36, 37, 39, 40, 45, 47, 51, 53, 56, 57, 61, 66, 67, 69, 73, 76, 91, 92, 93, 94, 97, 99, 100, 102, 103, 105, 114, 115, 116, 118, 119, 121, 122, 124, 127, 128, 130, 131
Milwaukee Auditorium 68, 73
Milwaukee, City of 6, 7, 22, 37, 39, 41, 50, 55, 60, 66, 68, 69, 72, 73, 101, 105, 109, 120, 131
Minnesota 67, 117
Mississippi
    Jackson 15
Modernism 5, 19
Moeller, Henry Archbishop 28
Montreal 77
Mooney, Edward Archbishop 67, 82, 83
Morris, Ellen 12
Morris, John B. Bishop 12, 14, 15, 17, 28
Mount Mary College 53, 63
Muench, Aloysius Archbishop ... 37, 40, 43, 44, 47, 52, 67, 110, 111, 122
Mundelein, George Cardinal 37, 71, 73, 81, 82, 83, 87, 88, 93
Mundelein Seminary 22, 115
Munich Crisis 71
Murphy, Dennis J. 25
Murphy, Francis 45
Murphy, Peter 65
Mussolini, Benito 69

N

Nashville, Chattanooga, and St. Louis Railway 11
Nashville, City of 6, 11, 12, 15, 29
Nashville, Diocese of 6, 12, 13, 15, 17, 24, 26
National Catholic School of Social Service 31
National Catholic Social Action Conference 68
National Catholic Welfare Conference (NCWC) 67, 70, 71
National Conference of Catholic Women 64
Nazi (National Socialism) 69, 70, 71, 72
Neo-Scholasticism/Neo-Thomism 5, 21,

22, 63
New Coeln, City of 100
New Deal 51, 68
New Jersey 7, 89
New Orleans, Archdiocese of 70
Newton, William 109, 110
New York, Archdiocese of 81, 82, 90, 93, 110
New York, City of 70
North American College 4, 7, 14, 16, 17, 18, 19, 20, 78, 82, 83, 84, 85, 93, 107, 108
Northwestern Mutual Insurance Company 42
Nova Scotia 6, 76, 104
Novena of Our Lady of Sorrows 103
Novena to Our Lady of Victory 103
Nuremburg Laws 70

O

O'Brien, William J. Archbishop 17, 90
O'Connell, William Henry Cardinal 129
O'Connor, William P. Bishop . 94, 114, 116, 122
O'Hara, Edwin Vincent Bishop 68, 99
Ohio 6, 15, 17, 28, 33, 58
       Cedar Point 16
       Mount Washington 16
Ohio State University 53
Old St. Mary's (Milwaukee) ... 100, 105, 114
O'Neill, Charles 47
Operation Doorbell 119
Ottaviani, Alfredo Cardinal 107
Our Lady of Mount Carmel (Kenosha) .. 58
Ozaukee County 120

P

Padre Pio of Pietralcina 116
Paray-le-Monial (France) 115
Patterson, Diocese of 90
Paulus, Francis 102

Peoria, Diocese of 20
Perry, William Tyler ... 34, 45, 49, 50, 94, 96
Philadelphia, Archdiocese of 17, 82, 84
Philippines 55
Pio Nono School 4, 65, 98
Pius XII, Pope 108, 111
Pius XI, Pope 24, 62, 67, 68, 69, 71, 90, 107, 111
Pius X, Pope 19, 62, 115
Plunkett, St. Oliver 15
Plunkett, Thomas S.S.J. 15, 45, 94, 128
Poland 73
Pompilj, Basilio Cardinal 108
Pontifical Biblical Institute (*Biblicum*) 109, 111
Pontifical Commission for Russia 88
Precious Blood Fathers 12
Program of Social Reconstruction 67
Propaganda University (Urban College) 14, 16, 22, 78, 80, 107
Pro-Prefect of the Congregation of Propaganda 123
Punda, Raymond 103
Purcell, John Baptist Archbishop 13

Q

Quadragesimo Anno (1931) 68
Quasten, Johannes 100
Quigley, James Archbishop ... 78, 79, 80, 81

R

Racine, City of 39
Racine County 105, 120
Racine Dominican Sisters 58, 131
Radant, George 56
Rainer, Joseph 43
Ray, Sister Baptist O.S.F. 59
Reconstruction Finance Corporation (RFC) 91
Regensburg, Diocese of 109
Reineher. Sister Joan O.S.F 59

INDEX

Rerum Novarum (1891) 67
Respighi, Pietro Cardinal 24
Riedel, Louis 64
Rochester, Diocese of 16, 110
Rockford, Diocese of 83
Rodriguez, St. Alphonsus 114
Roessner, Clemens C.PP.S. 12
Rome 5, 6, 7, 13, 14, 16, 17, 18, 19,
    21, 23, 24, 35, 51, 53, 71, 75, 78, 79, 80,
    81, 82, 83, 84, 86, 87, 88, 90, 93, 94, 107,
    111, 120, 124, 130
Roncalli, Angelo 81
Roosevelt, Franklin D. 68, 91
Rossi. Raffaele O.C.D. Cardinal 90
Ruffini, Ernesto Cardinal 108
Rummel, Joseph Archbishop 70
Rummel, Leo, O.Praem 5
Ryan, John A. 67

S

Sacred Heart of Jesus 107, 114, 115,
    116, 118
Sacred Heart Sanitarium 101
Sacrorum Antistitum (1910) 19
Salesianum 110
Salotti, Carlo Archbishop 90
Santa Maria Sopra Minerva 108
Santa Susanna (Rome) 90
Schinner, Augustine Bishop 55
Schnitzler, Peter 106
School Sisters of Notre Dame 105, 106, 114
School Sisters of St. Francis 58, 101
Schrembs, Joseph Archbishop 34
Schwab, Philip 100
Seminary–Charities 122
Serra Club 111
Sheboygan, City of 39, 69, 122, 123
Sheel, Brother Maurelian F.S.C 26
Simeoni, Angelo 56, 57, 58
Sisters of St. Agnes 58, 105
Sisters of St. Francis of Assisi 59
Sisters of the Divine Savior 55

Sisters of the Precious Blood 12
Social Action Department (SAD) ... 67, 123
Sodality of the Blessed Virgin Mary 64
Sodality Union of the Milwaukee
    Archdiocese (SUMA) 64
Somerville, City of 76
Southeastern Wisconsin Planning
    Commission 119
Specialized Catholic Action 123
Spellman, Francis Cardinal 20, 81, 93
Spokane, Diocese of 55
Springob, Joseph 102, 121
St. Aemillian's Orphanage 37, 47, 49, 73,
    101, 102, 121
St. Agnes Church (Chicago) 81
St. Agnes Outside the Walls 24
St. Albertus (Dominican College) 60
St. Anne's Church (Milwaukee) 54, 97
Stark, Mother Celestine O.S.F. 59
State Normal School (Wisconsin) 59
St. Benedict the Moor (Milwaukee) 38, 131
St. Bernard's Home for Working Men 40
St. Bernard's Seminary (Rochester) 110
St. Boniface Church (Milwaukee) 72
St. Charles Boys Home (Milwaukee) 50
St. Clement's Church (Sheybogan) 123
St. Elizabeth Church (Milwaukee) 65
St. Francis, City of 4
St. Francis de Sales Seminary. 7, 37, 40, 43,
    67, 68, 106, 109, 110, 112, 115, 124, 129
St. Gregory's Seminary (Cincinnati) 15
St. James Church (Kenosha) 42
St. John University (Toledo) 33
St. Joseph School 37
St. Joseph's Church (Waukesha) 109
St. Louis, Archdiocese of 82
St. Mary's Academy (Milwaukee) 59, 60, 68
St. Mary's Hospital (Milwaukee) 7, 103
St. Mary's Seminary (Baltimore) 15, 78
St. Michael Priest Fund 49
St. Patrick Church (Memphis) 24, 25,
    26, 27

St. Paul-Outside-The-Walls (Rome) 97
St. Paul Seminary (St. Paul) 40
St. Paul Station (Milwaukee) 37
Stritch, Eugene Lewis 11
Stritch, Garrett 11, 12
Stritch, Katherine Malley 11, 12
Stritch, Samuel A. Archbishop 5, 6, 7, 10,
    11, 12, 13, 14, 15, 16, 17, 18, 19, 20, 21,
    22, 23, 24, 25, 26, 27, 28, 29, 30, 31, 32,
    33, 34, 35, 36, 37, 38, 39, 40, 41, 42, 43,
    44, 45, 46, 47, 48, 49, 50, 51, 52, 53, 54,
    55, 56, 57, 58, 59, 61, 62, 63, 64, 65, 66,
    67, 68, 69, 70, 71, 72, 73, 75, 91, 93, 94,
    96, 98, 99, 100, 101, 102, 110, 111, 112,
    115, 122, 123, 124, 127, 128, 130, 131
Stritch, Thomas (brother) 12
Stritch, Thomas (nephew) 27, 45
St. Rose Orphanage 47
St. Sebastian Church (Milwaukee) 99
St. Vincent de Paul Society 39, 47, 48, 65
St. Vincent Orphanage 47
Summer School of Catholic Action 68
Superior, City of 113
Superior, Diocese of 7, 55, 94, 104, 113,
    114, 116, 117, 118, 119
Supreme Council for the Propagation of
    the Faith 87
Surges, Frank 48, 65, 102
Switzerland 70, 100
Sycamore Mills Powder Company 11

T

Tanner, Paul Bishop 65
Tanquerey, Adolphe S.S. 114
Tardini, Domenico Cardinal 108
Temple Emanu-el (Milwaukee) 72
The Calaroga 60
The Spiritual Life (1930) 114
Third Baptist Church (Toledo) 37
Third Reich 70
Three Archbishops of Milwaukee 3

Tiry, Clara 38
Toledo, City of 28, 29, 31, 32, 35, 39, 56
Toledo, Diocese of 15, 28, 29, 31, 32, 33,
    34, 36, 37, 45, 50, 51, 58, 73, 128
Traudt, Bernard .. 37, 40, 52, 53, 54, 55, 109
Trenton, Diocese of 7, 73, 89, 90, 91, 92,
    93, 128

U

Ubi Arcano Dei (1922) 62
United Catholic Campaign 48
University of Wisconsin 3
Ursuline Sisters 33

V

Valparaiso (Chile) 115
Vatican Apostolic Archives 9
Vatican I 5
Vatican II 111, 127, 130
Via dell'Umilta 16, 84
Vianney, St. John 107
Vienna (Austria) 71
Villa Santa Caterina 19

W

Walsh, Thomas Bishop 89, 90
Walz, Maximillian 29, 30
Washington County 120
Washington D.C. 31
Waukesha County 120
Weakland, Rembert G. O.S.B.
    Archbishop 127
West Allis 106
White, Joseph M. 6
Whitfield, James 25, 28
Williams, Katherine 63
Wisconsin State Board of Control 113
Wisconsin, State of 3, 5, 6, 7, 10, 39, 100,
    105, 116, 117, 119, 122

World War I 67
World War II 7, 112, 116
WTMJ 49

Y

Young Christian Students (YCS) 66, 123
Young Christian Workers (YCW) ... 66, 123